KING ALFRED'S COLLEGE
WINCHESTER

To be returned on or before the day marked
below:—

PLEASE ENTER ON ISSUE SLIP:

AUTHOR   GEORGE

TITLE   Ill fares the land

ACCESSION No.   7857

Ill fares the land

Also by Susan George

How the Other Half Dies
The Real Reasons for World Hunger

Feeding the Few
Corporate Control of Food

Food for Beginners

ESSAYS ON FOOD HUNGER & POWER

Ill fares the land

Susan George

Writers and Readers

First published by

Institute for Policy Studies
1901 Q Street N.W.
Washington, D.C. 20009
USA

This edition first published 1985 in Great Britain by

Writers and Readers Publishing Cooperative Society Limited
144 Camden High Street,
London NW1 0NE
England

ISBN 0 86316 090 5

Printed and bound in Great Britain
by A. Wheaton & Co. Ltd, Exeter

The Institute for Policy Studies is a nonpartisan research institute.
The views expressed in this work are solely those of the author.

Ill fares the land, to hastening ills a prey,
Where wealth accumulates, and men decay;
Princes and lords may flourish, or may fade;
A breath can make them, as a breath has made.
But a bold peasantry, their country's pride,
When once destroyed, can never be supplied.

Oliver Goldsmith,
"The Deserted Village," 1770

Contents

Foreword

There is food in plenty, yet millions suffer from starvation and malnutrition. Hunger, the most unnecessary and intractable of human afflictions, continues to plague millions of human beings and to kill some 40,000 of them daily, mocking the efforts of two Development Decades and three World Hunger Years. This somber reality forces all who choose to see to understand the inadequacies of conventional wisdom concerning the causes and cures for hunger. Over the past decade, beginning as one of the organizers of a path-breaking report on world hunger issued at the 1974 World Food Conference, Dr. Susan George has been central to a small group of courageous scholars who have challenged reigning development shibboleths. Today, their ideas find increasing acceptance among all serious students, if not yet adoption by the development establishment.

Their first efforts were devoted to de-constructing the prevailing assumptions on hunger, demonstrating their empirical inadequacy and their hidden political assumptions. For example:

Hunger is caused by over-population. But as Susan George and her colleagues established, in country after country, food production can exceed population growth and hunger may still increase. Moreover, the concept of over-population assumes that someone has the right to define the measures of "adequate population," foreboding prerogative to be held by the distant powerful.

Hunger can be alleviated by food trade and assistance. Since the United States spends billions each day to bribe its farmers not to produce grain, many humanitarians believe that the United States and other grain exporters should simply feed the world. Yet, as Susan George demonstrates, humanitarian aid may be both necessary in emergencies and dangerous in duration. Dependency on food imports—either by purchase or by grant—is a precarious addiction for any people. Popular tastes in food are changed; indigenous skills are lost; local production undermined. And then when the supply is constricted—because prices rise or generosity lessens—withdrawal can be painful indeed.

Hunger is a scientific problem, which can be alleviated by technological innovation. The technical fix is still the dominant school in aid circles. Transferring pieces of the high production U.S. model—high-yield seeds, post-harvest technology (the current fad)—are said to increase production and offer the promise of ending hunger. But decades of technological fixes have had one rather consistent result: even where production has been increased, hunger has been its partner. As Dr.

George details, the U.S. "model" is wholly unsuited for most underdeveloping countries (and may be increasingly difficult to sustain in the United States itself). The transfer and promotion of technological solutions tends to increase inequality of power and wealth, concentrate land and resources in the hands of the few, displace the many. The result too often is more production by the few of crops which the many cannot afford to buy. Increasingly, the world witnesses countries in which one-third to one-half of the population is needed neither for production nor for consumption. Starvation is one end which awaits them.

The technological fix has a macroeconomic twin in the modern global economy. Development aid, international monetary assistance, transnational corporate investment are all geared towards integrating Third World economies into a global market. Country after country is encouraged to develop export industries—often in commodities—to gain the resources necessary for development. With few exceptions the results are deplorable: the best land is devoted to export crops and exported at prices controlled by others. An increasing portion of the foreign exchange earned must pay for food for consumption, also imported at prices controlled by others. When commodity prices drop, financial credits decline, imports must be reduced. The result is often starvation.

The second task of Dr. George and her small group of colleagues has been to outline an agenda for research and action to reconstruct an alternative knowledge about hunger. Hunger, they conclude, is a political problem, a problem of power and will. Scholars should study the poor less and the powerful more, seeking to find ways to lessen their power. Rather than enlist elites into a global modernized growth sector, countries might better find ways to empower the majority to increase their own resources. Hunger is a product of poverty, but if poverty is to be alleviated, systems of power and privilege will have to be challenged.

In this area, of course, Susan George's writings are the most prophetic and the most controversial. Elites do not generally sponsor challenges to their privilege. It does not pay scholars or development officials to challenge the powerful. Such temerity results in decreased budgets, insecure tenures, a drying up of research funds. Few have accepted the risk.

The result is that the same patterns are repeated over and over again. This year the Reagan Administration seeks $8.4 billion in economic assistance for Central America. Its stated purpose is to stimulate export-led economic growth. Central America is to become the Singapore and Philippines of the West. Anyone with even a passing knowledge of the region, however, is struck by the parallels with John F. Kennedy's Alliance for Progress. There, the Cuban revolution raised a "national security" concern with revolution in the hemisphere. There too, economic assistance and reform was to be accompanied by counter-insurgency and military aid—a "shield" behind which growth could occur. There too, economic aid was to foster export-led economic growth. In Central America, the growth of the global economy and the assistance of the United States led to unprecedented economic growth rates in the late 1960s and 1970s. In Guatemala, El Salvador, and Nicaragua, the result was the elites grew wealthier, and the poor majority grew poorer. Thousands were dispossessed of the small plots of land they cultivated; thousands were uprooted to cities where no employment was to be found. Political repression quieted their protests, until revolution once again swept the region. Now the same tragedy seems likely to be replayed.

This ignorance is not accidental. If scholars and development officials do not feel free to challenge the powerful, they will do little to transform the lives of the powerless. It is the extraordinary service of Susan George's insights and passion to expose this inescapable truth.

Robert L. Borosage
Director
Institute for Policy Studies

Author's Note

With the approval and the encouragement of the Institute for Policy Studies, I've decided to publish for a wider audience these papers, written between 1979 and 1982 under auspices which limited their circulation to small groups (the case, at least, for all but the two last, short chapters).

The chief reason for this decision is that visible famine is once again pushing the issues of hunger and underdevelopment into the forefront of public consciousness. It's not that hunger had ever gone away—it had merely receded from the television screen, due to the temporary absence of victims spectacular enough to photograph. Now, God help them, and us, the victims are back for all to see. Perhaps such needless suffering will at least compel *serious* discussion of their plight, and what might—must—be done about it. Such a debate should be carried on by as many people as possible, and, I would submit, forced upon those who do not care to participate, either from bureaucratic inertia or because it is not in their economic or political interests to do so.

With this book, I hope to contribute to such a debate. The pieces collected here all run along the lines of my previous work, i.e., they examine questions of *power*. Some fit into the 'food systems and hunger' category, others are more concerned with how we *think* about food systems and hunger; all deal with the means by which some groups gain authority and ascendancy over others. Control of the world food system—the subject of much of my earlier writing and of some that appears here—implies control over technology and ideology, scholarship and culture as well. Such areas are not peripheral to the horrors of hunger.

The reader will find, inevitably, some overlap. I have left repetitions whenever they seemed necessary to the arguments and provided a brief introductory note to each chapter that explains under what circumstances it was written.

Like many a Third World country, I shall never be able to pay back most of my debts. But here the usefulness of the capitalist metaphor ends, since my "creditors" have not asked for anything in return for their "investments," except that I get on with whatever appeared important to me to do. Thanks without measure, then, to two institutions and two people: To IPS/TNI for trust and for allowing me to mark, this year, the most fulfilling of tenth anniversaries as a Fellow and member of a true Fellowship. To the French Catholic Hunger and Development Committee (Comité Catholique contre la Faim et pour le Développement—CCFD) for extra financial help to pay working expenses—including my trip to Bangladesh—during most of the period in which these essays were written. To Pierre Spitz, for having long and generously shared his ideas, and been exactly on target in his criticism of mine. To the anonymous but no less esteemed woman who a year ago sent a check for my word processor, thereby changing my life. Now I wonder how I ever managed to type those endless drafts of the papers in this collection!

Lardy (Essonne), France
April 1984

Overcoming Hunger

strengthen the weak, weaken the strong

The Food and Agriculture Organization (FAO) of the United Nations proclaimed 16 October 1981 the first World Food Day and has now made it an annual event. FAO's objective is to promote widespread public knowledge and concern about food and hunger problems throughout the world, and to this end the WFD Secretariat commissioned several papers which were to be published in five or six languages and sent as a kit to the dozens of national committees to aid them in their observance of World Food Day. I accepted the Secretariat's invitation to write one of these papers and revised it several times to conform as closely as possible to the needs and desires of FAO. Although I accepted changes suggested by the World Food Day staff and avoided unfavorable mention of specific countries, publication was ultimately refused. I was told off the record by the kind and somewhat embarrassed editor I'd been working with that the piece was still too polemical and political for FAO's taste.

The Organization honored its contractual obligations to me and has graciously consented to publication here. The article appears in its final version (with only minor stylistic changes) as it came back from the Secretariat just before the final refusal. The reader must judge whether the latter was warranted.

Perhaps World Food Day calls for commemoration, but surely not celebration. How could one 'celebrate' a day on which as many as 40,000 people will succumb to hunger? Moreover, barring an unforeseen, major overhaul of the world's political and economic system, there is every reason to suppose their numbers will be even greater on 16 October 1982, 1983, 1984 . . . .

One hopes this observation might provoke first outrage, then inquiry, and finally, action. If 16 October is to differ from any other day, it will be because widespread observance of World Food Day helps significant numbers of people throughout the world move from indignation (without which there is no motivation) toward accurate analyses of the issues (without which there can be no effective action) and from this anger and understanding onward to organization and practical politics.

Relatively Small Amounts of Food Are Needed

Estimates of the number of severely malnourished people range from 450 million (FAO) to a billion (the World Bank). Experts agree that the relative and absolute numbers of hungry people have never been so high, and that they are increasing.

The 15 million children who, according to UNICEF's estimate, die prematurely each year from hunger or hunger-related illness *could* be saved by an infinitesimal portion of the food harvested in the world. Simple arithmetic demonstrates how this is so:

- There are about 3,500 calories per kilo of grain, so a ton supplies an average 3,500,000 calories.
- FAO says 2,300-2,400 calories a day are usually adequate for proper *adult* nutrition.
- We shall be extra careful and assume children should eat as much as adults.
- At 2,300 calories x 365 days, each child would thus need 839,500 calories a year, which means each ton of grain could provide for over four children (4.17, to be precise).
- A million tons would feed more than four million, and to provide

3.

all year long for all 15 million children who now die from hunger, we would need to count on just about 3.6 million tons of cereals altogether.

Does this sound like a lot?

It may, until you learn that world harvests in 1980 were 1,556 million tons of cereals. The share needed to save 15 million young lives is thus equal *at most* to a two-thousandth (0.002 percent) of global crops—a figure as ludicrously small as it appears to be tragically unobtainable. Even this tiny figure exaggerates, because we have not only assumed a high daily ration, but we've also proceeded as if no other resources existed besides cereals—not even breast milk.

We could apply the same sort of arithmetic in discussing food for the 450 million people FAO classifies as severely malnourished. Let's grant a very generous ration of 2,740 calories a day, or one ton of grain per 3.5 adults per year. We would arrive at 128 million tons of cereals required to wipe out serious hunger and malnutrition—8 percent of the world's most recent harvest, less than the United States feeds its livestock.

In practice, however, needs are much less, since we've assumed 100 percent dependence on these cereals—that is, 450 million people with zero resources of their own, who have neither fish nor fowl, root crops nor oil seeds, fruits nor vegetables, milk nor meat. A World Bank economist wrote recently that a mere 2 percent of world grain harvests would provide enough food for *over a billion* people who need it.[1]

Victims, Resources, and Crucial Questions

Showing how little food, proportionally, would be required to rid the world of hunger may help prompt indignation; unfortunately, it contributes very little to analysis. Numbers like the ones just given have three major drawbacks:

1. They mask the fact that the needs of poor people with no purchasing power do not create what economists call "effective demand." The poor cannot express their needs in terms of money, the only language the market economy understands. Food *ought* to be a basic human right. However, this right cannot be exercised in a system which divides people into two categories: those who can pay (called "consumers") and those who cannot.

2. These figures imply that the problem is "to feed" people. If only we could manage to divert X percent of our abundance, "we" could feed "them" and no one would go hungry. The problem, however, is to

make sure people can feed themselves. Given the opportunity, they will do just that; they will not need "us." Unfortunately, through no fault of their own, fewer and fewer people *can* feed themselves.

3. These numbers also concentrate on quantifying the victims (and the resources theoretically available to help them out). It's not that the victims are unimportant—but if we focus only on them, we shall lose sight of the really crucial questions:
   - *Who controls* food and food producing resources, especially land?
   - *Who decides* what constitutes the agricultural "surplus" and how it is distributed?
   - *Who has the power* to determine that some will eat while others will not?

A Question of Relationships

For a world so proud of its science, its technology, and its management skills, eliminating hunger should be child's play. Since it still exists, one logical conclusion is that hunger is not primarily a scientific, technical, or organizational problem.

Suppose we change the angle of vision? What if we consider, not the poor and hungry themselves, but their *relationships* to society, particularly to its powerful members, locally, nationally, and internationally? "Conventional wisdom" focuses on the victims of hunger and always sees them as people *lacking* something—food and money, of course, but also technology, skills, knowledge (and, in the worst cases, even intelligence). What if, on the contrary, we regarded these millions of poor people as a rich national resource who lack only *power*, the power to control their own environments and the circumstances of their lives? By up-ending it, we shall discover that the problem of hunger is not one of technology or organization but of politics; morally, the issue is not charity, but justice.

From Development to Underdevelopment

In former times, the least powerful people seem to have been better off than they are today, relative to the situation of the most powerful.

They have wine and spices and fair bread, and we have oat cake and straw and water to drink. They have leisure and fine houses; we have pain and labour, the rain and wind in the fields. And yet it is of us and of our toil that these men hold their state.[2]

This text, six hundred years old, is taken from a sermon preached during an English peasant rebellion in 1381. Has anything much changed? Yes—today, the really poor are found in different areas, and they may not even have "oat cake, straw and water to drink." One area in Asia is reporting deaths from exposure for the first time. Why? Because straw, with which the very poorest people cover themselves during the cold nights, used to be free. Now it has a price which they cannot afford. So they freeze.[3] Pure water to drink is the exception rather than the rule for poor Third World people. And how many would be glad to have oat cake or any other grain, along with labor of any kind, even in the rain and wind in the fields. While tragic famines could and did strike with awful regularity in precolonial times, historical and anthropological evidence suggests that poor people in the now "underdeveloped" countries once had far easier access to food than they have today.[4]

Throughout history, ruling groups have tried to keep a great secret: they need the peasants—the producers of wealth—far more than the peasants need them. Patron/client relationships in most "traditional" societies limit the exploitation to which peasants need submit and offer some security in times of hardship. Those who control land and other resources have responsibilities towards those who serve them. Self-interest opposes killing the goose that lays the golden eggs. As a result, in "traditional" societies, the peasantry survives in all but the most dire circumstances.

Today, however, patron/client arrangements nearly everywhere have broken down and have been replaced by capitalist relationships. Land, food, and human labor alike become nothing but commodities and sources of profit.[5] As a result, hunger is increasing in both scope and severity. Deprivation on today's scale is a thoroughly modern phenomenon. Humanity has taken several thousand years to reach its present stage of underdevelopment.

Candidates For Hunger

In many countries with serious food problems, at least a third of the rural population is totally landless. An additional third may exist on holdings of less than a hectare.[6] Both rural and urban unemployment are on the upswing, while the Third World labor force will likely increase by nearly half a billion before the end of the century.[7]

All these people are candidates for hunger. Instead of searching for the economic and political causes and implications of this drastic situation, many 'experts' focus our attention on the victims. We are told that people—the landless and the jobless—go hungry through their own fault, that they are pushing themselves off the farms and into unemployment; they are worsening their own plight because they have too many children.

Any analysis should, however, not only ask *why* the poor have children (risk-spreading, security, etc.)[8]—but also *who decides* how many is too many. *Who determines* what constitutes "over" population? "Over" in relation to what? In relation, no doubt, to some ideal level where available resources, including food, "balance" with the number of people who want to consume them.

In fact, where *does* the imbalance lie today? The rich countries (not quite 25 percent of world population) consume between two-thirds and three-quarters of the world's production, including its food production. Their animals alone eat nearly a third of all cereal grains harvested.[9]

While huge imbalances in consumption exist between rich and poor countries, the most perceptible gaps are those between the rich and poor citizens of developing countries. To predict levels of hunger and malnutrition in any country, one need look only at the degree of land concentration, the circumstances of tenancy, and the proportion of landless laborers. The more unequal the holdings, the more insecure the tenancies, the higher the proportion of landless people, the greater the incidence of hunger will be. When fewer than 5 percent of the landholders control 70 percent or more of the cropland (a commonplace occurrence); when tenants must pay exorbitant rents and are vulnerable to eviction at the landlords' pleasure; when large numbers of rural dwellers have only the off-chance of selling their labor power standing between them and starvation, then one need look no further for the immediate causes of hunger. If the first priority is to maintain this status quo, it is quite true that there are "too many" people.

Inequality Breeds Inefficiency

Inequality also severely limits the amount of food that can be produced. A number of studies have shown that smaller holdings produce more food than large estates.[10] When farmers have secure tenure and know the benefits of their labor will accrue to them and their families—not to a landlord, a money lender, or a middleman— then they will work very hard indeed.

A more just society is a better-fed society. When the rich take the best, large numbers of peasants must make do with a tiny proportion of second-best land. "Over" cultivation or "over" grazing results. When development experts ascribe such sins to small peasants and herders, their vocabulary focuses on the supposed wrongdoing of the victims, deflecting attention from the meager resources that the landholding minority allot to the poor majority.

When even "over" cultivation fails to ensure survival (for, of course, an environment limited both in size and in quality *does* deteriorate under population pressure), the alternative is migration to an already "over" crowded city.[11] Here the term "over" populated describes very precisely the unliveable Third World shanty-towns inhabited by desperate, displaced ex-peasants.

Development Games

Today, it has been officially recognized that gross inequalities contribute to hunger. Even the bland recommendations of international conferences now call upon governments to display the "political will necessary" to eliminate them. These resolutions do not, however, explain why governments whose supporters have a deep stake in the *status quo* would willingly destroy their own power base.

Governments—if we assume that they are genuinely concerned for the poor and hungry—will find that some development policies are easier to carry out than others. An analogy from game theory illustrates why. In a zero-sum game, if A wins, B must lose: all the points won and lost cancel each other out. Health and education are not zero-sum development games. If A earns his first degree certificate, B need not give up his Ph.D.; when C receives prenatal care, this does not imply that D will have a heart attack.* Indeed, when poor C risks catching a disease, then so does rich D. Dominant groups sometimes feel that environmental and health improvements are a necessity—and the poor benefit as a result. One Latin American country recently stamped out an epidemic by vaccinating 80 million people in ten months.[12]

An all-out attack on hunger is something else. Workable anti-hunger strategies strike landholding elites, and rightly so, as zero-sum games: if the landless and the small peasantry gain greater access to land, credit, and other food producing resources this must almost always be at the expense of those who presently control them. Therefore, one finds dozens of historical and contemporary examples of the wealthy's refusal to play any game at all—until violence becomes the only recourse of the deprived. It is thus logical that as landlessness and hunger increase, repression must also increase and that a part of the arms trade—estimated at 1 to 2 billion dollars annually—is devoted to weapons designed to quell internal revolts.[13] When uprisings

---

*This is not to say there are no problems of *budgetary* allocations between primary, secondary, and higher education, or between city hospital-based and decentralized health care.

succeed, hunger may decrease dramatically. In the single year following the victory of the Sandinistas in Nicaragua, basic grain production went up by fully one third, and was far more equally distributed.[14]

Strategies to End Hunger

Steps to alleviate hunger never take place in a social vacuum. Inevitably, a power structure is already in place. Advantages of any anti-hunger project or strategy are likely to flow toward better-endowed groups (in both industrialized and developing countries), unless stringent precautions are taken to ensure that the benefits actually reach the poor. Donor agencies and governments, however well-meaning, would thus do well to keep the following propositions in mind:

1. Development strategies benefiting the least favored classes (or nations) will not be acceptable to the dominant classes or nations unless their interests are also substantially served.
2. Development strategies which benefit *only* poor classes or nations will be ignored, sabotaged, or otherwise suppressed by the powerful insofar as possible.
3. Development strategies serving the interests of the elites while doing positive harm to the poor will still be put into practice and if necessary maintained by violence, so long as no basic change in the balance of political and social forces takes place.

Currently many people claim that the Brandt Commission strategy[15]—a massive transfer of resources from the industrialized to the developing countries—would end hunger and underdevelopment. They stress that this strategy is *not* a zero-sum game; that both rich and poor nations would ultimately benefit. Such reasoning is fine as far as it goes. It has the advantage of realism since it appeals to the self-interest of the rich nations—not to ethical principles. It stops short of asking how resources transferred will actually be shared with the worst-off. Three decades of failed "trickle-down" development should have taught us some skepticism on this point. And *even if* equitable sharing were to take place, there is no guarantee the Third World could achieve food self-sufficiency through resource transfer alone in the absence of major structural—even psychological—changes. Two formidable obstacles to ending hunger would remain: the "cash-crop imperative" and the "modernization syndrome."

Crops and Robbers

Many Third World countries have opted for a development strategy encouraging cash crops for export at the expense of food production. While some privileged groups may profit handsomely from prolonging such colonial production patterns or from introducing such non-traditional crops as fresh fruits, vegetables, flowers (plus livestock) for off-season delivery to northern markets, overall these countries have been swindled. For them, participating in the world market is like playing Monopoly against partners who begin the game with all the most desirable properties.

Tropical commodity prices fluctuate wildly and unforeseeably. The only predictable thing about them is that they decline constantly compared to the prices of manufactured goods poor countries must import. Of every $100 consumers spend on tropical products, in their final form, producer countries get only $15. The remaining 85 percent lines the pockets of those in industrialized countries—mostly transnational corporations (TNCs)—which control shipping, processing, and merchandising.[16]

Cash crops also hog scarce resources like fertilizers and credit; as a result food production inexorably declines. In turn, this must be compensated by importing increasingly expensive foods from abroad: in 1979-80, developing countries imported about 85 million tons of cereals.[17] (At the World Food Conference in 1974, FAO feared imports of 85 million tons in . . . 1985.) The Third World is thus in the unenviable position of exporting greater and greater quantities of tropical agricultural products at (falling) prices it does not control in exchange for greater and greater quantities of vital foodstuffs at (rising) prices it does not control either. This is one manifestation of power relations at the international level. The victims are entire nations, particularly the poorest among them. Fairer and more stable prices for cash crops (as recommended by Brandt, UNCTAD, etc.) are necessary, though not sufficient, conditions for an effective anti-hunger strategy.

Modernization: Remedy or Disease?

Most countries, however, can't get off the trade treadmill even when they recognize the danger, because they must repay their crushing foreign debt, now estimated at $400 billion.* Thus they continue to submit to unequal exchange in the marketplace. This is a fairly straightforward kind of exploitation. A more subtle aspect of the control dominant countries exercise over their poor Southern neighbors can be described as the "modernization syndrome."

---

*It has doubled to $800 billion in the three years since this paper was written.

Victims of this syndrome assume that the agricultural practices of industrialized countries (especially North America) are the most "modern," the most efficient and consequently the most desirable. These techniques are, in fact, often seen as the *only* way to improve output in countries whose agriculture is considered, by comparison, backward.

North American agriculture is of dubious "modernity," even on its home ground, as a good many Western experts are beginning to recognize. It consumes enormous amounts of expensive, non-renewable energy, much of it in the form of manufactured inputs. It depletes and pollutes the environment through poor conservation practices, land and water "mining," overuse and run-offs of agricultural chemicals.[18] Farmers have fallen under the control of non-producers—giant corporations that provide inputs and buy the produce, enormous banks that furnish costly financial credit. While this agriculture appears to be immensely powerful and productive, yields per hectare in the United States of all the major food grains have stabilized or fallen since the early 1970s.[19] Most important of all, the North American system grew up under unique historical conditions which included a vast frontier and relatively few people to farm it. Consequently, the whole thrust of this agriculture has always been to obtain the greatest possible yields *per person*, not *per unit of land*.

Conditions in most developing countries are exactly the opposite: they have relatively small amounts of arable land per person and vast numbers of rural people who need employment. What could be less "modern"—if eliminating hunger is the goal—than to model development or a system expressly designed to substitute fossil fuels and industrial products for work done by people? No wonder Third World rural unemployment is on the rise.

"Modernization" downgrades the potential contributions of peasants' practical knowledge to improving production. If Western recipes for development were abandoned, peasants, now perceived as "obstacles" to development, could occupy their rightful place as intelligent farmers and sources of agricultural knowledge.[20]

Because "modernization" implies extensive use of very expensive inputs, wealthier farmers benefit most. They may indeed increase their production (just as the corporations that sell such agricultural inputs increase their profits), but this increase may actually *contribute* to hunger.

That hunger will automatically diminish when food production increases is a common but naive assumption. Higher productivity—and higher profits—actually mean more hungry people when they bring evictions, foreclosures on debts so owners can control more land, more labor-saving machinery, higher rents, higher prices for land, lower wages for growing numbers of available laborers, etc.[21] When

11.

governments neither subsidize nor protect smaller cultivators and market forces are left free play, the weak will lack access to the "modernization package." They will be eliminated when agriculture becomes more a way of making profits than of feeding people—as happens all too often in "modernized" systems. The problem is not improved technology *per se*, but to whom it is available.

Dependency is Undependable

A country cannot be independent when it depends on the goodwill of rich consumers to keep on buying its coffee or its fresh strawberries even in periods of economic crisis and spending cutbacks. Nor can it be free when it depends on TNCs for pricing, processing, and marketing its agricultural products; or on the wealthy countries for vital foodstuffs, or on food aid; or on foreign funds to finance these imports. Landless laborers and poor cultivators at the bottom of the Third World ladder cannot win when they depend on the diminishing goodwill of their richer, better-endowed local neighbors who hold literal life-and-death power over them and their families.

When concerned citizens and those professionally responsible for confronting problems of hunger and underdevelopment face up to a few unpalatable truths, we may then make some headway:

1. That all governments are concerned for, and representative of, the majority of their people is patent nonsense. Plenty of governments are most concerned with enriching those who keep them in power. Human rights, including the right to food, run a poor second.

2. Very little is to be expected from most industrialized countries (except that they will encourage dependency). Food aid decreases as need increases and prices rise. Socialist industrialized countries contribute a far smaller proportion of their GNP to development aid than capitalist countries whose own record is, for the most part, dismal. The only way to get more help from such bastions of national selfishness is to convince them it is in their interest to aid poor countries (as the Brandt Commission attempts to do).

3. The present world capitalist order sanctions private ownership while taking no responsibility for those who own nothing. It has been incapable of setting upper limits for accumulation of riches by an individual, a corporation, or, for that matter, a nation. By contrast, the lower limit—death by hunger—is very clearly defined. For a world economy ruled by competition and the profit motive, millions of people are utterly useless. From capital's viewpoint, they are not needed for food production—machines and chemicals will do as well—and they are not even needed for consumption so long

as enough consumers with purchasing power will reliably upgrade their diets in value (more animal products, more off-season, expensive perishables), thus ensuring continued profits. In food systems dedicated to *eliminating* labor, poor people are a drag on the economy, not the asset they would be if labor-*intensive* food systems were designed.[22] World capitalism would prefer that such "useless" people disappear—at present, starvation is one avenue towards this end.

Conclusion: Some Suggestions for Action

For international organizations and governments to become more effective in acting against hunger, they must receive considerable help—some of it in the form of criticism and pressure—from concerned citizens all over the world working through their own non-governmental organizations (NGOs). Here are some major goals. The first two are politically the most difficult to achieve; the others more immediately feasible.

- Wipe out Third World debt. Without relief, countries can't even make a choice between food crops and cash crops. This would, among other things, mean that rich countries would have to pay off their own banks.
- Limit development aid and projects to countries whose leaders have demonstrated their concern for their own poor through real land reform, income redistribution policies and the like. No rewards for those countries where aid reinforces the repressive capacity of an already dominant, and rapacious, class.
- Increase food aid—but only for emergency purposes. Institutionalized food aid has consistently discouraged local production and sidetracked governments from undertaking serious reforms and cereals policies.
- Insist on more socio-economic research about the effects of past, present, and future development projects and strategies on the worst-off. Few agencies welcome independent evaluation of their work—an indication that such is needed.
- Continue to push for the basket of measures summed up in the "New International Economic Order." The NIEO wouldn't eliminate hunger, but it would at least allow governments to plan more rationally.
- Help NGOs that sponsor small projects directly beneficial to peasant communities aimed at increasing local self-reliance and greater popular control over resources.

- Support alternative agronomic and ecological research that rejects conventional "modernization" in favor of improving *local* systems in the context of *local* environments. Treat the peasantry as a source of knowledge, not as an obstacle to progress.
- Accept new technology selectively, and only when it enhances local solutions, ultimately reducing dependency.

We should encourage whatever measures help local or regional food systems protect peasant self-sufficiency and reduce their vulnerability to outside pressures. Conversely, we should reject incorporation of local food systems into larger, more powerful ones directed by the richest countries for their own purposes. To do this, we must find available political spaces and work in them, and we must create new ones. Hunger will never be vanquished unless we can strengthen the weak, and weaken the strong.

Notes

1. World Bank, *World Development Report 1980*, Washington, D.C., August 1980, p. 61. See also Marcelo Selowsky, *The economic dimensions of malnutrition in young children*, World Bank Working Paper 294, 1978, Table 1. Selowsky assumes, as we have done, 3,500 calories per kilo of grain.
2. John Ball, The Sermon at Blackheath, 1381, cited in Leonard Silk, *The Economists*, New York, Discus Books (Avon), 1978, pp. 230-31.
3. Personal communication from a member of the Indian Administrative Service, New Delhi.
4. See, for example, Dr. Moises Behar (WHO) "Nutrition of Mayan children before the Conquest and now," *Clinical Pediatrics*, Vol. 9, 1970, pp. 187-88, as well as contemporary testimony cited in Nicole Ball, "Understanding the causes of African famine," *Journal of Modern African Studies*, Vol. 14, No. 3, 1976; Pierre Spitz, "Silent Violence: Famine and Inequality," in *Violence and its Causes*, UNESCO, 1980; Fray Bartolomeo de las Casas, *Très Brève Relation de la Déstruction des Indes*, Paris, Maspèro, 1979 (original 1552).
5. For some aspects of the breakdown of 'patron/client' relations, see Prof. Shigeru Ishikawa, *Labour Absorption in Asian Agriculture*, Bangkok, ILO (ARTEP), July 1978, sp. p. 96 f. and Appendix 3. Many instances of this breakdown are described in the series of volumes published by the UN Research Institute for Social Development under the general title "Social and economic implications of the large-scale introduction of new varieties of foodgrains" but more simply described as the "Green Revolution" series. The director of the project, the late Andrew Pearse, published an overview volume containing many details on the "crisis of livelihood": *Seeds of Plenty, Seeds of Want*, UNRISD and Oxford University Press, 1980.
6. World Bank, *Land Reform*, Rural Development Series, July 1974, sp. Tables 6, p. 55 and 11, p. 60. The Bank's figures are old; landlessness and rural dispossession have grown much worse during the past decade. One should also consult the collective volume *Poverty and Landlessness in Rural Asia*, ILO, 1977.
7. World Bank, *World Development Report 1979*, Ch. 4, "Employment Trends and Issues," and the same report for 1980, p. 40. See also *Poverty and Landlessness*, op. cit.
8. For details on the population issue, see Susan George, *How the Other Half Dies*, Montclair, N.J., Allanheld, Osmun, 1977, Ch. 2.
9. National Research Council, *World Food and Nutrition Study*, Washington, D.C., National Academy of Sciences, 1977, Table 1, p. 157.

10. World Bank, 1980, op. cit., p. 42 ("Small is productive"); also World Bank, 1974, op. cit., Table 2.2, p. 32.

11. In the 1960s, between 30 and 70 percent of the additions to urban population were migrants from rural areas. World Bank, 1979, op. cit., p. 55. Rural out-migration has accelerated since the 1960s under 'Green Revolution' and 'modernization' pressures: see the UNRISD series and the Pearse overview, op. cit.

12. World Bank, 1980, op. cit., p. 72.

13. Michael T. Klare, "The international repression trade," *The Bulletin of the Atomic Scientists*, November 1979, and with Cynthia Arnson, *Supplying Repression*, Washington, D.C. and Amsterdam, Institute for Policy Studies, 1981.

14. The increase in Nicaraguan basic grain production is clear from figures the author consulted in January 1981 in Managua at the Research Center attached to the Ministry of Agriculture (INRA-CIERA). Small peasants had, for the first time, access to land, credit, fertilizer, etc., and massively improved their food production. There is a drawback: since people are well fed for the first time in decades, they are much less anxious to earn wages by harvesting cash crops—this has posed a problem for the government.

15. Report of the Independent Commission on International Development Issues—consistently referred to as the Brandt Commission: *North-South: A Programme for Survival*, London, Pan, 1980.

16. FAO, World Conference on Agrarian Reform and Rural Development, INF.3, "Examen et analyse de la réforme agraire et du développement rural dans les pays en voie de développement. . . ." 1979, Ch. 11, pp. 112-13.

17. FAO, *The State of Food and Agriculture 1979*, FAO, 1980, pp. 1-54.

18. A growing literature on the environmental/energy impact of the North American food system includes Robert van den Bosch, *The Pesticide Conspiracy*, Garden City, N.Y., Doubleday, 1978; *Farmers' Use of Pesticides* (in 1964, 1971, 1976) US Department of Agriculture Economic Reports Nos. 145, 268, 418; David and Marcia Pimentel, *Food, Energy and Society*, Resource and Environmental Science Series, London, Edward Arnold, 1979; Gerald Leach, *Energy and Food Production*, Guilford, Surrey, IPC Science and Technology Press, 1976; Nicole Ball, "Deserts bloom . . . and wither," *Ecologist Quarterly*, Spring 1978. The impact poor conservation practices may have on US exports (and vice-versa) is examined in Lauren Soth, "The Grain Export Boom: Should It Be Tamed?" *Foreign Affairs*, Spring 1981.

19. See Sylvan Wittwer, "Food Production Resources: land, water, energy, fertilizer, capital and manpower" in *Plant and Animal Products in the US Food System*, Washington, D.C., National Research Council, National Academy of Sciences, 1978, sp. pp. 23-25.

20. Pierre Spitz has frequently insisted on the importance of peasants' contributions to agricultural knowledge and "scientific" neglect thereof: see, *inter alia*, "La recherche agronomique au service des paysans pauvres du Tiers Monde" in *Revue Tiers Monde* (IEDES-PUF) Vol. XX, No. 78, April-June 1979, and "Livelihood and the Food Squeeze," *Ceres*, FAO, May-June 1981.

21. See the UNRISD 'Green Revolution' series, op. cit.; and K.C. Abercrombie, "Agricultural employment in Latin America," International Labour Organisation, *Review*, July 1972.

22. It is instructive to note that China has consistently *added* agricultural labor at a rate of about 2 percent per annum since 1952, while the growth rates of net output per worker have climbed from 2.6 in 1952-57 to 8.3 in 1977-79. See World Bank, *China: Socialist Economic Development*, a "Grey Cover," i.e., restricted report, No. 3391-CHA, Annex C, pp. 72-73, 1 June 1981.

Dangerous Embrace
culture, economics, politics, and food systems

In late 1979, the United Nations Economic Commission for Europe (ECE)—including both Western and Eastern Europe—held a joint seminar with the UN Environment Programme (UNEP) on "Alternative Patterns of Development and Lifestyles" (Ljubljana, Yugoslavia, 3-8 December 1979). The seminar was attended, inter alia, *by "senior advisors to ECE governments on environmental problems" and part of the discussion was devoted to relationships between ECE countries and the Third World. The UNEP and ECE Secretariats commissioned a certain number of background papers, including this one. My editor for this contribution was (quite properly) demanding: this resulted in an unusually high proportion of footnotes to text, and it's possibly the most closely argued paper in this collection. The language is not UNese, but it is as neutral as my language ever becomes. The paper is reproduced here with the kind permission of the Secretariats of the ECE and of UNEP.*

Culture, Economics, Politics and Food Systems

Every food system—defined as the totality of tangible and intangible means employed by a given human community for the production, conservation, distribution, and consumption of food—has profound effects on the environment. There is no such thing as a "natural" ecosystem; each one is shaped by the cultural perceptions, economic arrangements and political confrontations of human beings in their efforts to assure themselves of this most basic human necessity. It is, furthermore, impossible to look at food systems as closed, static entities. Not only are dynamic historical processes occurring within each society to transform them (and with them, the environment) but interactions between food systems in different parts of the globe are taking place with increasing frequency and intensity. The result is that these systems, in most parts of the world, are today wide open. As the secretariat of this seminar has noted:

> Countries of the world are closely linked through the mechanisms of international economy, political, scientific-technological and cultural relations and exchange, as well as through the environment. Events and actions by one country . . . have repercussions and impacts on others, on the international community as a whole and on the biosphere.[1]

This is nowhere more true than in the realm of food, but in order to understand the full magnitude of the impact of changes in food systems today, we would do well to examine first some of the processes which have shaped our food systems and environment in the past. It is not merely physical factors but culture, economics, and politics that are the prime determinants of food systems and the environment in which they exist.

Cultural Impact on the Environment

Ecologists study patterns of plant/animal species development; some take into account the impact of human farming techniques on these patterns, but few note that the way people use their environment for subsistence is dictated not only by the *physical* capacity

19.

of that environment to sustain certain kinds of plants or animals but also by the view the community has of its own nature and its relationship to the rest of the universe. Diets in fact represent a cultural—even ethical—*choice* among the range of foods that are physically feasible in a given environment.[2]

It is impossible to account for the ecological differences between southern Spain and northern Morocco without contrasting Catholicism and Islam. The original ecosystems of these areas were virtually identical from a "natural" point of view, and yet were utterly transformed by people who, if they were Moslems, needed large numbers of sacrificial sheep, but did not eat—and therefore hunt—wild boar any more than they drank wine. Catholics, on the other hand, terraced their hillsides with vineyards and raised a variety of animals (eating a variety of plants) and hunted the wild boar to near extinction.[3] Quite evidently flora and fauna are not the whole story.

Our physical surroundings, the aspect of our landscapes can thus be "decoded" as incarnations of culture. But the above examples of the impact of food/cultural systems on the environment are still relatively simple because they have been confined to specific geographic areas and self-contained human communities where the pace of historical transformation and conflict was relatively slow.

Economic and Political Pressures on Food Systems

In contrast, prolonged or intense interaction with *outside* food systems will accelerate the processes of history; changes wrought in a community's original food system may have unforeseeable consequences to the point where that community may lose control over its own environment. These changes may involve the use of superior force to oblige one group to devote its land and labor to satisfying the needs of another (agricultural tribute, colonization); or they may be introduced peacefully and yet have violent consequences.

The effects of introducing a single hitherto-unknown plant or animal species into a new environment can be immeasurable. Could Philip Miller, Curator of London's Chelsea Physic Garden in the eighteenth century, know that he would lay the foundations for a whole new mode of life (and, as has been submitted, for a Civil War) when he sent the first packet of cotton seeds to the recently founded American colony of Georgia?[4] When Christopher Columbus took the first specimens of sugar cane to the Antilles in 1495, who would have predicted that great maritime and commercial empires would be based on the sugar trade and that Africa would be ravaged to provide slaves for Caribbean plantations? Ships carrying slaves out to provide labor for sugar or cotton economies, furthermore, brought back new plants from the Americas on the return voyage—among them groundnuts, corn, sweet potatoes and manioc—all still mainstays of African diets.[5]

In our time, the introduction of large-scale commercial soybean cultivation in Brazil since the 1960s has, in a remarkably short period, altered land-use patterns over vast areas. This has reduced the availability and raised the prices of staple foods for the average Brazilian and had important, generally negative, consequences not only for nutrition but for small business and levels of employment. Black beans, once the staple protein source for poor Brazilians, have recently been in such short supply due to preferential land use for soya cultivation that riots have occurred at city supermarkets; municipal elections in Rio de Janeiro produced a huge write-in vote for *feijaos*.[6]

The use of superior force to alter food systems to one's own advantage is a more straightforward case whether such force is exercised by the dominant class in a particular society or by outsiders over another country. Recurrent problems for governments everywhere are feeding the populations of the cities (if they are not fed, mobs may riot and sometimes overthrow the rulers) and, secondly, acquiring enough cash for national treasuries to maintain civil and military bureaucracies (as well as provide some luxuries for the elite that form their power base). The countryside must therefore be controlled and the peasantry kept in line lest it refuse to provide the surplus necessary to these ends. Needless to say, this "surplus" is rarely perceived as such by peasants themselves, who are always the first to go hungry. Thus it is not surprising that food was routinely exported from pre-revolutionary France, even in times of famine, nor that agricultural exports from the Sahel actually *increased* during the recent severe drought and food crisis.[7] Economic, political, and, where necessary, military pressures brought to bear on one class by another are thus vital determinants of food production and distribution.[8]

Colonization: From Abundance to Scarcity

Superior force is also exercised at the international level; the most obvious case is that of colonialism. Empires throughout history have commandeered another people's food supplies (e.g., the Roman use, and eventual exhaustion, of North Africa as a granary). The colonial empires of modern times ushered in a new phase, however, by using colonies to furnish the "cash-crops" that fuelled their own industrial development; they thus became architects of radically different food systems and environmental transformers on a huge scale.

Societies that now suffer endemic food shortages were, on the whole, food-abundant societies in precolonial times. Dr. Moises Behar has, for example, shown that the Mayans, prior to the Spanish Conquest, had no serious nutritional problems. They ate corn, beans, fruits, vegetables, and game meat; they cleared land, farmed it briefly,

21.

then let it revert to jungle, thus preserving the ecological balance and soil fertility.[9] With the Conquest came malnutrition—not only because the Spaniards took over the crops and sold them back to the Indians for gold, but also because they forced them to clear land for cotton, sugar, and coffee.

European travelers to Africa in the sixteenth, seventeenth, and eighteenth centuries often noted the prosperous agrarian life. One of them recorded the response of an Ethiopian peasant to his amazement at the food abundance: "Honoured guest, do not be amazed . . . if it were not for the multitude of locusts and hail . . . we should not sow the half of what we sow, because so much remains that it cannot be believed. . . . (Even if all these plagues came at once, there would still be food reserves). . . . We have no scarcity."[10]

Closer to our own time, we have the word of a French colonial inspector who wrote to his Government in 1932 on his mission to famine-stricken Upper Volta:

> One can only wonder how it happens that populations . . . who always had on hand three harvests in reserve and to whom it was socially unacceptable to eat grain that had spent less than three years in the granary have suddenly become improvident. They managed to get through the terrible drought-induced famine of 1914 without hardship. (Although their stocks were depleted, they were soon able to reconstitute them, at least until 1926, a good year for cotton but a bad one for millet.) Since then, these people, once accustomed to food abundance are now living from hand to mouth. . . . I feel morally bound to point out that the intensification of the policy giving priority to industrial products has coincided with an increase in the frequency of food shortages.[11]

The Inspector has here put his finger on the causes of hunger: not drought, hail, or locusts—environmental hazards which peasants took into account and had learned to cope with—but enforced cash crop production for metropolitan countries. Just as the early Spanish colonizers in search of cash crop products pushed American Indians onto soil-poor and easily eroded hillsides where their descendants still live, so was much subsequent dislocation in previously efficient food systems directly induced by commercial interests backed by national ones—the ancestors, one might say, of today's transnational corporations (TNCs). A few examples of such dislocations follow.

In the first decade of this century, the British Peruvian Amazon Company recruited hundreds of employees to "organize the collection and portage of rubber to river stations by thousands of natives. . . . The means of coercion used against them included the withholding of food by driving them from their subsistence plots and thus rendering them

22.

dependent upon foodstuffs imported by the Company . . . possibly thousands lost their lives from hunger and murder."[12]

Similar events occurred in the Belgian Congo on a larger scale: "Since the conquest, difficulties in recruiting workers hampered colonization: it was necessary . . . violently to expropriate the peasants from their collective landholdings. . . . Mercilessly crushing the old African agrarian system, the finance companies proceeded to make gigantic expropriations, seizing millions of hectares, burning villages . . . forcing [the people] to gather plantation crops at gunpoint."[13]

French methods were sometimes more subtle but had the same destructive results for local food systems. Taxation was the chief coercive instrument employed; it gave peasants no choice but to produce groundnuts or cotton for sale to French companies. Taxes were demanded even in periods of acute famine (itself engendered by cash crops, as seen above). As the French Governor of Niger said to a subordinate who had informed him that there was neither money nor food in his district in the famine year 1931: "I wish you to be less lenient and, on the contrary, expect you to hasten the collection of taxes owed by those under your jurisdiction."[14]

This is the framework created by the earlier interventions of industrialized countries in Third World food systems. It is the setting in which today's development efforts must take place. An analysis of the contemporary situation requires that a further dimension be added, as it is now recognized that our planet is a global system and that there is no chance of Third World food systems reverting to relative autarchy. They must try to evolve towards a new, different, yet viable, equilibrium starting from a historical situation basically unfavorable to them.

Authentic Food Systems versus the Dominant Model

One goal of any national development policy should be to arrive at a food system which (a) is environment enhancing and ecologically sustainable, (b) provides enough foodstuffs at reasonable cost to the entire population, including the poorest strata, for a nutritionally-balanced diet while remaining consonant with its cultural preferences and (c) provides great enough quantities to insure national food self-sufficiency, as a guarantee against outside political manipulation through food aid or exports.

Let us call such an ideal food system "authentic," drawing etymologically on *authentès/authentikos* as Greek for "one who does anything by his own hand." An "inauthentic" system would, therefore, be one directed by outside hands; usually, such a system cannot satisfactorily feed its own people (though it may be efficient at feeding outsiders). In the contemporary world, there is competition between food systems; the model of the industrialized countries is now dominant and this model is being exported as a solution to development problems in the Third World. However, food system models are in fact non-exportable: any successful development of authentic food systems will have to be based on local bioregions and local solutions, on a cultural renaissance, and a scientific upgrading and enrichment of locally accumulated knowledge and techniques.

There are naturally many gradations along a continuum of authenticity/inauthenticity. One system can remain authentic while incorporating elements from another, but only when it does so on its own terms. Unfortunately, there are few historical or contemporary examples where both systems profit through mutual, beneficial incorporation. Note that the authentic food system has been defined as one serving the entire population. It is, of course, quite possible that the dominant class of a system may have something to gain from either self-reliance or inauthenticity. The physical resources of all but the smallest Third World countries (and perhaps even theirs) are sufficient for attaining authenticity. The obstacle is, rather, the permeable nature of their food systems and their vulnerability to outside pressures.

While outright imperial violence is now rarely used to alter a developing country's food system (and may tarnish the prestige of states that use it), detrimental forces are still at work. To make clear the nature of these forces, and in support of the proposition that the industrialized countries' dominant model is being exported, we must see how and why this model itself developed. The point of the exercise is to show its costs and diminish its prestige—a prestige which gives this model a psychological advantage directly influencing decisions made in the Third World. Countries though nominally independent may still be colonized both economically and intellectually. This state of affairs is often promoted by industrialized countries which have a short-term interest in keeping the Third World dependent on their agricultural methods, processes and products, and in maintaining an international division of labor in which the southern hemisphere continues to supply cheap traditional cash crops as well as, increasingly, luxury agricultural products to northern markets. The rich countries may also, consciously or unconsciously, regard their own achievements as the only viable solutions for problems posed elsewhere.

This combination of forces creates a three-fold and self-sustaining dependency. First, Southern countries accept and practice an imported food system model, requiring expensive inputs, as a supposed avenue towards development. Second, this model proves incapable of solving their food problem and thus fosters increased food imports. Third, to pay for these imports, agricultural export production (using, again, costly, imported techniques) must be increased, thus reducing resources devoted to the attainment of an authentic national food system. And so on, in a vicious spiral.

What, then, is the nature of the dominant model? For the sake of clarity, one can show a food system as a line composed of three segments:

	AGRICULTURAL PRODUCTION	POST HARVEST ACTIVITIES
INPUTS ——————▶	——————▶	
including physical inputs, research and financial credit		including storage, processing and distribution

These categories can be considerably refined; they nevertheless apply to the means employed by any human community for feeding itself. In the now developed countries, the first and last segments of the line have come entirely under the control of industry (often called "agribusiness"). This development has made it meaningless to speak in classic economic terms of the primary (agricultual), secondary (industrial), and tertiary (services) sectors at a time when agriculture has itself become entirely dependent both on industrial products and on services (like bank credit and transport) both upstream and downstream from the farm.

Historical Development of the Dominant Model

The historical conditions of countries where the high-technology (HT) food production and distribution system developed made it an entirely rational and effective response to the problems posed in these societies. In the United States, for instance, vast land areas coupled with limited manpower made early mechanization imperative—indeed agricultural productivity in the United States has *always* been measured in terms of output *per man*, not per unit of land. By the 1850s, tens of thousands of machines were already used in America. Harvesters were most popular because they insured the farmer against disaster and helped him spread his risks. With a harvester, he could reap crops on as much land as he could sow—impossible if he relied on hand cutting. An inventive explosion of agricultural technology—all of it labor saving—took place in the nineteenth century: steel-share moldboard ploughs, drill planters, mechanical screws for land clearing, barbed wire allowing enclosure of much larger areas in a shorter time, and grain binders were a few of the

25.

items, besides harvesters, enjoying widespread use in the latter half of the century. The Civil War, which took so many men away from farming, the emancipation of slaves and the burgeoning industrial development creating a demand for factory workers all strengthened the trend towards HT agriculture.

The desired results were soon manifest: in 1800, 373 man-hours were needed to produce 100 bushels of wheat and 344 man-hours for the same amount of corn. By 1900, the figures were reduced respectively to 108 and 147. But by 1959, the necessary man-hours were only 18 and 22.[15] The first agricultural revolution in the now-industrialized countries consisted in a shift from human to animal-mechanical power. The second revolution, which has taken place especially since World War II, is based on scientific innovation and automotive power. It has reduced labor input even more drastically through the use of self-propelled machinery, genetically improved varieties and much greater amounts of fertilizers and pesticides.

The HT model is today capable of feeding 220 million Americans through the efforts of fewer than 2.5 million farmers and of producing millions of tons for export besides. There is no question that it has been successful. There is no question either that this model is generally regarded throughout the world as the most "modern" and "efficient" ever devised. This is true enough—but only for those countries whose specific needs are met by it. The United States was land-rich and labor-poor. Nearly all today's developing countries are land-poor and labor-rich. A production system entirely conceived to economize labor and spare workers for other tasks will have the same consequences when used in countries whose chief unresolved dilemma is to give productive employment to the great majority of the population that lives in rural areas yet cannot find a livelihood there. Countries which adopt such a model must, therefore, expect it to contribute to labor displacement and to encourage out-migration towards already unmanageable cities where few jobs in industry or services are available. On these grounds alone, there is reason to question both the "modernity" and the "efficiency" of the HT model when applied to the Third World.

Costs of the High Technology Model

There are other serious costs—economic, social, and environmental—inherent in this model also. It is so expensive to use that only the most competitive farms stay in business: just after World War II, US farmers spent half their gross incomes on production expenses; the figure is now 80 percent and rising. Farm supplies are a $90 billion annual business and borrowing to purchase them has resulted in $120 billion agricultural credit outstanding. To sustain the cost/price squeeze, farmers must try to expand at the expense of their less fortunate neighbors. Four and a half million family farms have been eliminated since the 1930s and today, one third of all food produce is supplied by a mere 2 percent of farmers grossing over $200,000 yearly, while the top 20 percent raise 80 percent of all crops and animals.[16] Land concentration is expected to continue: one US Department of Agriculture scenario predicts that by 1985, over 60 percent of all farmers working in 1975 will have disappeared.[17] It now costs about $400,000 to create a single job in agriculture, approximately ten times the cost of an average job in industry.

The struggle to survive imposes a goal of maximum yields today— whatever the long-term costs. Monoculture and economies of scale become the only answer: a farmer cannot afford to leave space for trees, hedges, pastures, fallow fields, or "low-value" crops. A detailed description, impossible here, of the ecological damage wrought by this system would include the increased use of fertilizers with rapidly diminishing returns; disastrous pest outbreaks (e.g., the cotton boll worm) created by pesticide use which destroys natural predators, and the pollution of land, water, and the rest of the food chain by these chemicals. Non-renewable energy to keep this system functioning amounts to 1,400 liters of oil per American per year. If one attempted to feed the world's 4,000 million people an American diet using US agricultural production technologies (assuming oil were the only energy source) all known petroleum reserves would be exhausted within eleven years. Underground water reserves are being "mined" for irrigation to the point that one reservoir, currently supplying seven States, will, at present rates, have disappeared by the year 2000. A third of US topsoil has already been irrevocably lost.[18]

Perhaps most alarming of all is the narrowing of the genetic base of North American crops. The devastating US corn blight in 1970 prompted a study by the National Academy of Sciences which concluded that North American crops are "impressively uniform genetically and impressively vulnerable." A mere six varieties of corn account for nearly three quarters of all production, two varieties of peas for 96 percent, four breadwheats for 75 percent of all Canadian harvests, etc.[19]

When we examine the post harvest segment of this "modern" and "efficient" food system, we find that it is incapable of providing a balanced diet to the entire population at a reasonable cost. The negative health aspects of the so-called "affluent diet" are too well documented to need elaboration here.[20] What is perhaps less well known is that malnutrition and outright starvation were so prevalent in the United States in the late 1960s that a federal crash program in food assistance was undertaken. Its cost to taxpayers is presently close to $10 billion annually, and one could argue that the United States could not long sustain a post-harvest system subservient to a highly concentrated food processing industry without subsidizing the poorest consumers. About three quarters of all profits realized in this sector go to some fifty companies; they benefit both from the sale of highly elaborated products to the majority of consumers as well as from food assistance programs. The latter are "backed by the American food industry which is strengthened by a substantial boost in purchasing power." Even so, several million hungry and malnourished Americans, especially in rural areas, do not receive the food assistance to which they are theoretically entitled.[21] A similar analysis of European food systems (themselves much imbricated in that of the United States) would yield similar conclusions.

We have, then, a food system which is neither environment enhancing nor ecologically sustainable, costly yet incapable of providing a nutritious diet for all the citizens of one of the wealthiest countries on earth. Its production system may—for the moment—be effective, but it is also scientifically crude and linear, relying on industrial techniques to yield an end-product (the system's only goal) that will fetch the best price on national and international markets. It is based on the survival of the fittest and elimination of all but the largest producers. Yet this is the system that more and more Third World countries are adopting—or attempting to adopt—because their dominant classes see it as more remunerative for themselves; or, to give them the benefit of the doubt, because they mistakenly equate "Western" with "productive" and "superior." The prestige of the HT model has grown highest in the developing countries at the very time significant numbers of knowledgeable Americans and Europeans are questioning the economic, social, and ecological relevance to national needs of their own systems; and particularly questioning the oligopolistic control agribusiness exerts over them.

The Interaction of the High Technology Model and Third World Food Systems

We have described the HT model, for the sake of convenience, as if it were closed, but we have already seen that no food system (even, or especially, a dominant one) is self-contained. The industrialized countries' system could not function without substantial inputs from the Third World—in fact, luxury supplements to Northern diets are more than ever provided by countries that themselves have a serious food problem.

Among possible objections to the above analysis are these three:

1. At the factual level, one might argue that the Third World is not adopting the dominant food system model, nor is it continuing to supply outside food systems, along colonial lines, on unfavorable terms.

2. Assuming that developing countries are adopting the dominant model, the negative consequences described have only recently become serious. Forewarned is forearmed: these negative aspects can be foreseen, counteracted, and mastered. In any event, the only way to conquer hunger is to increase food production, and the only way to do that is to modernize agriculture in ways that have proven effective in the industrialized countries.

3. The role of bilateral and multilateral assistance is to help Third World governments attain the development objectives they have themselves defined, and modernization along dominant model lines is what they want. It is not in the province of donor governments or agencies to contradict them.

Concerning the first objection, I have attempted elsewhere to show in some detail that the Third World is in fact adopting the dominant model as well as supplying its supplementary food needs on unequal terms.[22] Suffice it here to summarize some major points.

The Third World as a Market for the HT Model

The Green Revolution strategy is a text-book case of the industrial input-intensive method of agricultural production. It should have been clear from the outset that only the better-off Third World farmers with access to credit would be able to adopt it and that small producers would find themselves at an immediate competitive disadvantage. This is exactly what has happened. Competition for land has increased as agriculture has become a profitable investment and rural dispossession has, as a result, intensified. The outcome is that while food production has indeed increased (although less than often claimed) fewer people proportionally are able to buy it and millions have been deprived of the means of producing food for themselves.[23]

Such effects were perhaps not intentional, but this commercialization of agriculture was certainly encouraged, as one US planner noted:

The agricultural modernization (the Green Revolution) seeds signal could be the seedbed of new market economies in the world's low income countries . . . [Green Revolution Farms must] make economic ties to a wide array of agribusinesses—manufacturers of agricultural equipment and chemicals, storage and warehousing operations, processing firms and distributing organizations. . . . Businessmen from the more developed economies and international lending agencies are all engaged in efforts to . . . spread the use of the new technologies.[24]

Mechanization is not, strictly speaking, necessary to Green Revolution husbandry, but it is often perceived by larger landholders as an effective means of social control and preferable to dealing with potentially restive agricultural laborers. Many governments' policies, particularly in Latin America, have directly encouraged mechanization, with the result that by 1972 2.5 million jobs had been lost on that continent alone, according to a "conservative estimate" by an FAO expert.[25]

The Green Revolution has also had the effect of reducing drastically the genetic variety of cultivated species in the Third World—thus increasing vulnerability to disease and eliminating part of the germ-plasm resources upon which all countries must rely for genetic improvements in the future.[26]

Large centralized storage and processing facilities for cereals and oilseeds on the industrialized country pattern are increasingly favored by lending agencies (and TNCs). An FAO expert paints this picture:

> Piles of rice bran rot in a government rice mill. Groundnut mills set up as outlets for farmers' crops stand idle because of lack of supplies. A grain marketing board operating grain stocks . . . finds that it must add 100 per cent to its purchasing price to cover all costs and losses incurred. Another board sends soldiers to induce farmers to sell their grain. . . . Further examples could be cited in the livestock, meat and dairy sectors. Most of these operations were initiated and implemented in developing countries with the assistance . . . of bilateral or international expertise. . . . What went wrong?[27]

His answer is that the realities of local economies are not considered; post harvest losses increase (in transport or through quickly spreading infestations) while the cost added to food by centralized storage and processing is at least 20 percent. Family or village level storage and processing is far less wasteful and less costly.

But foreign food processing firms typically gain returns on investment averaging 14 to 16 percent in Latin America (doubtless more in Africa and Asia) as compared to 4 to 6 percent in developed countries.[28] This gives them an obvious incentive to produce in the poorer countries where labor is cheap and generally unprotected by trade unions. They then tend to siphon off local raw materials for processing the same kinds of high-value-added products they manufacture in rich countries. The promotion of baby formulas, bringing increased infant mortality and malnutrition in their wake, is one of the best known examples,[29] but soft-drink, breakfast cereal, snack food, and other processors have all found lucrative markets in the Third World. The role of TNC advertising firms is crucial in this regard.[30] Animals are increasingly fed with grain suitable for human beings—or with feedstuffs grown on land previously devoted to food crops. Hatcheries, ranches, and even beef-cattle feedlots are now among the preferred investments of TNCs.[31]

The Third World as Supplier of Northern Food Systems in a Context of Uncertainty

On the supply side, developing countries are now providing industrialized country markets not only with traditional tropical cash crops but more and more with luxury goods like meat, fish, off-season fruits or vegetables, flowers, and even pet foods. Traditional Third World exports are declining in relative importance and value. Taking 1967 as a base year with an index of 100, US Imports of tropical products reached all of 101 in 1977. But the US Index for "supplementary" imports (i.e., animal or vegetable products that can also be raised in temperate-zone countries) was 165 in 1977. Total US imports of supplementary products were valued at more than $6 billion in 1977, and over 50 percent of these products came from developing countries. Poorer nations of Latin America or Asia now supply 20 percent of US meat imports and over 70 percent of the imported vegetable products.[32] Similar trends are apparent in Europe, for which Africa is the chief supplier of off-season luxury produce, frequently grown by peasants under contract to TNCs.[33]

Meanwhile, agribusiness TNCs are developing strategies for reducing their own dependence on tropical products from the Third World. Substitutes for jute and cotton are already widely used, while industrial use of sugar is gradually giving way to high-fructose corn syrup. It is now even possible to produce coffee and cocoa substitutes from plentiful temperate country crops like soya or barley. A shrub which gives natural latex as good as the *hévea*'s is being grown experimentally. Higher prices for tropical crops (negotiated in fora like UNCTAD) will encourage recourse to substitutes, so that exporting countries have no guarantee they can sell the same quantities as before, even if they gain concessions on prices.[34]

The Third World is more than ever a supplier of food products at prices it does not control and a purchaser of staple foods (70 million tons last year) at prices it does not control either. A bushel of US wheat which cost $3.12 in late August 1978 sold for $4.30 in September 1979. As a whole, the Third World now buys about 30 percent of all American agricultural exports—and up to 60 percent of that part of the US wheat crop that is sold abroad.[35] "Comparative advantage" as a doctrine for development seems to have become bankrupt—except for the rich countries.

Increasing Production: A Solution?

Let us take the second possible objection—that one can guard against harmful effects of the dominant food system model; production must, in any case, be increased. The relevant question here is "Production for whom?" In our present system, production is indeed being increased, but much of it is going to the already well fed, because purchasing power is the magnet that draws food, both nationally and internationally. Through the dominant model, income and capital are concentrated in industrialized countries and in the hands of a Third World minority. It might be possible to guard against negative trends (although I do not believe it possible in market economies); what is evident is that such precautions have not been taken to date. Agrarian reform has made little progress, land ceiling legislation is not applied; while "the market," i.e., competition, allocates access not only to food but to food producing resources, including land.

Powerful commercial interests have a stake in promulgating the dominant model, either to sell agricultural products and expertise or to produce exportable agricultural goods more cheaply than they can do in rich countries. These interests are frequently aided by governments and by the UN system itself. Tied aid is one mechanism encouraging dependency on an imported model. The largest bilateral donor (the United States) ties 73 percent of its aid, while the OECD Development Assistance Committee countries as a group tie over half of theirs.[36] American food aid is legally conditioned by the recipients' acceptance of Green Revolution-type techniques, while the European Development Fund gives over half its agricultural assistance to cash, not food crop projects.[37] The US Government's Overseas Private Investment Corporation supplies loans and political risk insurance to agribusiness companies' projects in the Third World, generally producing for export or for the monied elites of poor countries. Until recently, over a hundred TNC agribusinesses were integrated in FAO as the "Industry Cooperative Programme."[38] Although the Director-General of FAO disbanded the ICP in 1978, it has regrouped and obtained consultative status with the UN Development Programme. In spite of such state or international agency support, no evidence has yet been supplied that TNCs contribute to authentic food systems.

Has the Third World Had a Real Choice of Food Systems?

The third possible objection—"this is what the developing

countries want"—brings us back to the problems of economic and intellectual colonization and to the responsibilities of developed countries. Decades of interference and technology transfer have resulted not only in economic dependency but in a transfer of values and attitudes as well. The dominant model is what the Third World "wants"—or may have been obliged to accept—because no one, with the exception of a few imaginative non-governmental organizations with no stake in dependent development, is offering anything else.

Northern governments and multilateral donors tend to finance the kinds of projects they understand (based, necessarily, on their own food systems) and those which will bring an immediate tangible return (in the form of traditional or luxury cash crops or purchases of inputs and expertise). This is, however, an extremely short-sighted policy on the part of donors whose own economic and political futures will be partly determined by the nature of the development process in poorer countries. The Iranian revolution was, for example, partly a violent reaction against the foreign takeover and large-scale destruction of a national food system which had resulted in the forcible displacement of several hundred thousand rural people and annual food imports costing half a billion dollars (from the United States alone)—this in a country which had once been self-sufficient.

Is There a Realistic Development Policy Alternative for Industrialized Country Governments?

Third World governments which accommodate easily to dependency and inauthentic food systems may not be in power forever, but those who replace them will tend to have long memories concerning those outside influences which either helped or harmed their nations. Despite recent historical examples of the violent rejection of dependency, it is nonetheless realistic to assume that most industrialized country governments will prefer to support Third World economic partners doubling as political allies. Real development always implies gains for some and losses for others (at least temporarily) and many Northern governments would probably find the political costs of undermining some of the interests of Third World elites that presently support them too great. Rich countries also back the activities of their own corporations, consulting firms, etc., which, as we have seen, find considerable profit in interference in Third World food systems. Thus governments would have a good many difficulties in altering their development policies so that they might bring greater benefits to the majorities of poor and hungry people. It is normal that States act on considerations of political power and economic advantage; they cannot be expected to behave altruistically nor respond to moral exhortation. This being said, it is still important to be somewhat "utopian." Governments are not monolithic; the role that particular individuals and agencies can play in reshaping at least some aspects of policy should not be discounted. Let us indulge, then, in a "conditional idealism" and venture onto the problematical ground of the possible, rather than confining ourselves to the pessimism of the probable. Assuming the developed countries are interested in lessening Third World dependency, how might they help southern hemisphere food systems evolve towards greater authenticity?

A Re-examination of Industrialized Countries' Consumption Patterns

First of all, rich countries would need to carry out a self-examination, facing squarely the situation in which their own past or present practices and demands have placed the developing countries. This would involve a critical look at the way their own consumption patterns influence land use and investment in the Third World. They should particularly try to discourage the relatively recent, so less entrenched, production of luxury foods (the aforementioned off-season vegetable products, meat, fish, and pet-foods) produced on some of the Third World's best agricultural land; and which contribute marginally if at all to the well-being of developed country citizens. This might be done by placing heavy import taxes on such items.

The New International Economic Order (NIEO), particularly as it concerns fairer and more stable prices for tropical commodities, would not of itself create authentic development, partly because incremental revenues would accrue mostly to dominant groups; partly because of the substitution phenomenon discussed above. It should, nevertheless, be supported, because it would provide the only means available for Third World governments to plan land and resource use more rationally. At present, they are devoting huge areas and heavy investments to cash crops because "boom and bust" cycles make this structurally necessary. That is to say, when the price of commodity X rises, producing countries (which have no mechanisms for consultations among themselves) try to grow more of that crop to take advantage of this price. When these unconcerted actions result in a glut—as they eventually do—the producing countries still try to grow more so as to keep their revenues stable in the face of falling prices. The NIEO, properly applied, could have the result of diminishing the area used for cash crops which are today more a part of the problem than a part of the solution.

Food Aid Policy

Since direct food assistance represents a high proportion of total development aid, a thorough examination of the impact of past policies should pay particular attention to it. Stepped-up food aid in the Sahel has, for example, had a number of negative consquences. It has resulted in taste-changes prompting huge increases in wheat and maize demand (+234 percent and +207 percent respectively between 1965 to 1967 and 1975 to 1977) whereas local wheat production covers only 2 percent of requirements. In a recent report to an intergovernmental conference called by the Club du Sahel and the CILSS (Permanent Inter-State Committee on Drought in the Sahel); an FAO expert spoke of the "desire for bread" and pointed out that:

Due to changes in feeding habits, the outlets available to traditional cereals remain limited and the incentives to increase production are small. In such a context, food assistance appears to be an easy solution, enabling urban populations—or privileged groups—to be supplied at relatively low prices, but failing by this very fact to achieve self-sufficiency in the matter of food supplies. . . . Whereas Sahel States have granted, since the sixties, priority to the extension of . . . groundnuts and cotton and have sometimes achieved spectacular success . . . it cannot be said that any real cereals policies have been implemented so far.[39]

Much the same could be said for other major food aid recipients like Bangladesh where donations rarely reach the people most in need, but whose sale to the better-off provides a substantial part of the national budget. Food assistance has frequently been specifically geared to increasing subsequent cash sales (this objective figures, for example, in the text of the US 'Food for Peace' law). Industrialized countries must determine whether they choose to aid themselves (by getting rid of surplus or increasing commercial food exports), political/military 'clients' (who will in turn sell the food aid to their own clientele), or populations which are truly at risk. If authentic food systems are the goal, policies stressing short-term, disaster-related food aid and direct relief for the poorest would be much more beneficial than the present long-term institutionalized programs. Low cost food imports should never be allowed to compete with local food production and thus to destroy local incentive.[40]

The Case for a Temporary Reduction in Development Aid Funding

The suggestion of a temporary reduction in development aid is, perhaps, the ultimate heresy, and as such would doubtless be seen by Northern governments as a political liability (or an easy alibi) and by Southern ones as another proof of First World selfishness. But there is ample evidence that present levels of aid are actually accelerating rural polarization, especially landlessness and loss of employment, because

35.

so much of it accrues to the higher strata of Third World societies.

Even conclusive evidence that certain development projects would cost less and have a much greater positive impact on poor local people will not prevent the adoption of their exact opposites. Comparative cost/income calculations showed in 1974, for example, that for oil palm development schemes in Nigeria, if "based on village processing units, growers' family incomes would be approximately 50 per cent higher and over-all investment in transport and processing facilities 75 per cent lower than in a large-scale industrial scheme."[41] The World Bank nonetheless made loans in 1975 and 1978 totaling $95 million—for large-scale, centralized industrial oil palm development in Nigeria.[42]

The cynical view of such activities is that agencies dominated by First World governments will encourage dependency by promoting projects relying on equipment procurable only from industrialized countries. A somewhat more charitable opinion would hold that lending agencies are (or at least want to be) permanent institutions and are thus obliged to spend huge sums of money, even if they worsen the position of the poor, because they must dispose of this year's budget in order to secure next year's. One would like to recommend, with little hope of being heard, a brief moratorium on aid combined with much higher spending on research (and a commitment to accept the policy implications of that research.)[43]

A brief hiatus could institute much longer time scales for project implementation. There is now much talk of "local participation," but few agencies are willing to allocate the necessary time for detailed research and necessarily complex consultations. Real participation would even entail, in many cases, the building up of rural organizations in order that their members might speak out without fear of reprisal from powerful local interests. Despite their crucial role in food production, processing (and sometimes marketing), rural Third World women are the most forgotten group of all, possibly because most development planners are men. Schemes that do not take women's specific skills and problems into account deserve to fail. Unfortunately, they sometimes "succeed" by making women's lives even harder.[44] Time "lost" in obtaining popular participation, including that of the lowest social strata and women, would be made up in time gained in effective project implementation. If the rural poor are convinced they have something to gain from a project, they will act as fast as any agency could wish, but they will quite properly resist "modernization" from which only the better-off groups (or only men) stand to benefit.

Lower cost projects, relying on a high labor content, are furthermore the only ones that stand a chance of replication throughout the country as a whole. It may be possible to create developed "pockets" by saturating a small area with capital and personnel, but such islands have little significance for the economy of the country as a whole and merely increase inequalities because they are too costly to generalize.

Recognizing the Relativity of Industrialized Country Food Systems

This is a complex recommendation because it runs counter not only to entrenched interests but also to entrenched mentalities. Industrialized countries should nonetheless try to re-examine the axioms of their development policies in order to accept the cultural, economic, and environmental relativity of their own food systems, as outlined above, rather than continue to think of them as panaceas for radically different societies. If this relativity could be accepted, it would amount to an intellectual revolution and could bring the goal of authentic food systems closer. If the industrialized countries could view their own systems not as universally applicable, but as local solutions to local problems and conditions, they would, simultaneously have an effect on decision makers in poorer countries—helping to rehabilitate the prestige of local solutions in these countries as well.

The introduction of the dominant food system has pushed Third World countries towards the kind of homogeneity which now prevails in industrialized countries; e.g., hyper-specialized monoculture and reduced genetic variety; commercially-induced food habits encouraging the consumption of identical products throughout the world (bread where no wheat is raised, soft-drinks, infant formula, etc.). The structural homogeneity of the developed countries' food systems is masked by an end product exhibiting great commercial pseudo-variety (e.g., one observer recently counted 85 different kinds of bottled salad dressing in an American supermarket). But this variety is spurious and controlled in reality by a very few firms using diverse labels made "different" through advertising.

Traditional Third World food systems may, on the contrary, be characterized by relative monotony of diet (broken by festivals and feasts) but be based on wide genetic and species heterogeneity. One Philippine tribe practicing shifting cultivation is able, for example, to identify and use 1,600 different plants. In one part of Tanzania, peasants cultivate 24 different kinds of rice; other examples of this empirical knowledge of species could be cited.[45] Traditional cultivation systems are also founded on heterogeneity—mixed cropping of trees, bushes, standing plants, and even certain "weeds" which play a positive protective role. Such techniques are time-tested responses to risk: homogeneity is vulnerable, but diversity is resistant and risk-spreading. Systems breakdowns are far more likely under conditions of structural homogeneity (blights over large areas, as have occurred in the Philippines and Indonesia—not to mention the Irish potato famine or the US corn blight). Monoculture is linear, seeking a single product year after year and paying the price in industrial inputs. Traditional systems are circular and return to the land what has been taken from it.

Peasants, left to themselves and given enough physical space, are environment improvers. The first farmers did not follow Ricardo's principles by using the best land first (it was beyond the physical capacity of the farming group, mostly women, to clear it) but the more easily worked terrain. As Professor Michel Cépède notes, "Fertility is progressively built up on naturally poor land."[46] Even today, in poorer countries, small plots worked by peasants have proved up to thirteen times as productive as large mechanized holdings,[47] although this is no longer possible when the resources available to them are drastically reduced. Then they are accused of "overcultivating" and "overgrazing" the little that has been left them—as indeed they must if they hope to ensure immediate survival.

Even if we take a country like Tanzania, generally regarded as striving for autonomous development, we find peasant knowledge neglected and significant inroads made by the dominant model. "Maize plantations as monocultures are considered a symbol of progress. In reality they present a great danger to soil fertility."[48] No one is studying the agricultural practices of the Tanzanian peasants, who cultivate 24 varieties of rice, although grants can be obtained for work on imported rice hybrids. Limestone powder from the major cement works is thrown away, whereas it could make excellent fertilizer—and chemical fertilizers are imported. As a Heidelberg University team working on improved agricultural methods reports on Tanzania:

> Until now, there has been nothing available except the strategy of high-yield varieties, fertilizers, pesticides and mechanization . . . A country like Tanzania which has decided to obtain independence even with economic disadvantages should be interested in [alternative "ecofarming"] methods. This is not yet the case; the influence of foreign advisors supporting the ideas of the Green Revolution, considering only the interests of industrial countries, is still too strong.[49]

What, then, must the influence of the "advisors" be in countries far more open to neocolonial influences than Tanzania? Local practices in some areas have been all but blotted out and absorbed by colonial or postcolonial cash crop production. In such areas, their resurrection would demand a veritable archeology of rural traditions. Elsewhere, there are better possibilities to collect, collate, and codify local knowledge, but few local or outside agencies and institutions take an interest in such activities.

Let us make quite clear that we are not advocating a "Garden of Eden" approach; suggesting a return, pure and simple, to ancestral methods, nor an artificial polarization with peasant practices at one extreme and industrialized country methods at the other. Peasant practices represent very real knowledge—not always easily accessible to outsiders—which has ensured food supplies for generations. But they are not perfect: they should be regarded as perfectible. Inputs from other food systems can be beneficially incorporated in these practices, but it should be the community itself which decides how and when. Mechanization, for example, can cause unemployment, but in a different social context it can also increase employment when used (as in China) to raise the number of possible yearly plantings, clear new land, etc. Whether outside elements are beneficial or harmful will greatly depend on the balance of social forces—and thus ultimately on the structures of power.

Isolated, generally ill-funded scientific work is being undertaken on the best "mixes" of peasant empirical knowledge and Western scientific techniques, but the creation of a new body of knowledge combining the two is still in its infancy. As one researcher has said: "Agricultural research in developing nations has been conditioned by cropping systems of the more developed countries [so] little attention has been paid to indigenous cropping systems . . . It is the lack of knowledge of the principles underlying mixed cropping that has prevented the application of improved technology to these farmers." One can, however, now show scientifically that indigenous cropping systems use labor more efficiently, give more stable yields from year to year and are "intrinsically higher yielding" than monoculture. "The subsistence farmer has developed a highly sophisticated system . . . based on good economic sense."[50]

Such systems, because they are based on high labor input, are the only ones that could employ the many willing hands now idle in the Third World, as they are the only ones that could serve as a basis for authentic food systems at the national level because they are less costly, replicable, and maintain ecological balance. Unfortunately— and this is a crucial drawback—they contribute very little to any- one's immediate profits—except for the local communities that employ them.

The Real Interests of Industrialized Country Governments

It is obviously not enough to point out the harmful effects of present policies, nor to propose more ecologically and socially rational ones so long as donor governments do not see their own interests served by a change. Ultimately, such governments have something to gain, even commercially, from more progressive policies, less subservient to short-term economic interests. Mahbub ul Haq of the World Bank explained this vividly:

> The [New International Economic Order] is not a one-way street of benefit only to the developing countries. Any new deal, whether it is negotiated nationally or internationally, ultimately must insure the viability of the entire society . . . My own favourite parallel is the comparison with the New Deal in the United States in the 1930s. What it did was to elevate the working classes from their status of dependency and uncertainty to a status of greater partnership in management by arranging a more equitable sharing of profits . . . I am sure that at the time, the people who ran corporations in the United States thought that President Roosevelt was a raving maniac and that the New Deal spelt the demise of capitalism. But with hindsight, one can see that it was an act of unparalleled leadership which saved the American system from its inner contradictions.[51]

Such arguments apply as well to the help the industrialized countries could given Third World governments in progressing towards authentic food systems. Improving rural prosperity for all—not just privileged groups—would increase demand for all kinds of goods. A distinguished American economist has shown, for example, that more stable prices for Third World commodities instituted ten years ago would have resulted in economic gains for the United States of $15 billion over the decade in prevented unemployment and GNP loss.[52]

Northern governments could also promote mutually beneficial trade by concentrating on writing off Third World public debt. In some cases, up to a third of export revenues returns immediately northward as annual debt-service. Debt reduction could be an alternative to direct funding of projects.

If developed country governments took the lead in necessary economic restructuring, if they were the first to point out the intrinsic value of local food systems, Third World governments might begin to take a renewed pride in their own cultural inheritance. If donor countries trained their own aid cadres and scientists to start from and build upon the local situation, rather than to alter it along industrialized-country lines, local cadres and scientists might begin to see their own peasantries as an indispensable and precious resource rather than as an obstacle to development as is so often the case today.

There will be formidable pressures against First World cooperation in the development of authentic Third World food systems. Some pressures will come from within—from the interests that have a financial or ideological stake in dependency. Some will come from without—from elements among Third World elites desirous of maintaining systems that cater to their needs or whims at the expense of their poorer compatriots. Yet a politics of vision should look towards a farther horizon; towards that diversity and authenticity—cultural and agricultural—upon which depends our common prosperity and survival.

Notes

1. Ljubljana ECE-UNEP Seminar document: ECOSOC/ECE/SEM.11/PM/R.1, October 1978, para. 10, mimeograph.
2. An example of culture and ethics setting dietary practice is to be found in the Jewish dietary laws. They particularly serve to distinguish categories which are, and must remain, separate: through food, man is distinguished from God, one people from another, the clean from the unclean, etc. For the Hebrews, anything mixed or partaking of two natures is unclean and thus inedible—be it a wingless bird, a water creature without scales and fins, or an animal both herbiverous and carniverous like the pig. The principle of separateness also applies to processes of food production, as in this passage from Leviticus: "Thou shalt not let thy cattle gender with a diverse kind, thou shalt not sow thy field with mingled seed." (XIX: 19). See Jean Soler, "The dietary prohibitions of the Hebrews," *The New York Review of Books*, 14 June 1979, pp. 24-30; and Mary Douglas, *Purity and Danger*, London, Routledge & Kegan Paul, 1966, Ch. 3.
3. Philip Stewart, "Human Ecology: a new kind of knowledge?" Paper presented at the colloquy, "Homme biologique et homme social," Centre Royaumont pour une Science de l'Homme, December 1978, mimeograph. An obvious example is the impact of Hindu beliefs on the Indian environment (the famous 'sacred cow').
4. Lesley Gordon, *Green Magic*, London, Ebury Press, 1977, p. 87; and for the connection between cotton and the Civil War, Gavin Wright, *The Political Economy of the Cotton South*, New York, W.W. Norton, 1978, Ch. 5.
5. Pierre Spitz, "Notes sur l'histoire des transferts de techniques dans le domaine de la production végétale," paper presented at the OECD seminar "Science, Technology and Development in a Changing World," DSTI/SPR 74.75, April 1975.
6. Centre Français du Commerce Extérieur, *Le Développement de la Production du Soja au Brésil*, Collection, 'Enquêtes à l'Etranger', November 1973, p. 49 f. See also UPI dispatches "Rio beans shortage causes disorders" and "Black beans the write-in choice of thousands who voted in Rio," in *The International Herald Tribune*, 13 October 1976 and 22 November 1976.
7. World Bank, *World Tables 1976*, Table 8, "Foreign Trade Structures: Export Composition," and Economic Data Sheet No. 1, "National Accounts and Prices."
8. Pierre Spitz has discussed this question at length in "Silent Violence: Famine and Inequality," *International Social Science Journal*, Vol. XXX, No. 4, 1978.
9. Dr. Moises Behar, "Nutrition of Mayan children before the Conquest and now," *Clinical Pediatrics*, Vol. 9, 1970, pp. 187-88.
10. Addis Hiwet, "Ethiopia: from autocracy to revolution," Occasional Paper No. 1, *Review of African Political Economy* (London), 1975, cited in Nicole Ball, "Understanding the causes of African famine," *Journal of Modern African Studies*, Vol. 14, No. 3, 1976, p. 522.
11. From French colonial archives in Laurence Wilhelm, "Le rôle et la dynamique de l'Etat à travers les crises de subsistance," unpublished *Mémoire de Thèse*, cited in

Spitz, "Silent Violence . . ." op. cit.

12. Andrew Pearse, *The Latin American Peasant*, London, Frank Cass, 1975, p. 9.

13. M. Merlier, *Le Congo de la colonisation Belge à l'Indépendence*, Paris, Maspéro, 1963, cited in M.K.K. Kabala Kabunda, "Multinational corporations and the installation of externally oriented economic structures in Africa" in Carl Widstrand, ed., *Multinational Firms in Africa*, Uppsala, 1975, pp. 305-6.

14. Le Gouverneur Blacher to the Administrateur du Cercle de Dosso, Niger, 16 June 1931, cited in J. Egg, et al., *Analyse descriptive de la famine des années 1931 au Niger et implications méthodologiques*, Paris, Institut National de la Recherche Agronomique, July 1975, mimeograph, p. 37. Jean Suret-Canale in *Afrique Noire*, Vol. II, *L'Ere Coloniale*, discusses the use of taxation in detail.

15. Various aspects of the development of the US model will be found in Alan Olmstead, "The mechanisation of reaping and mowing in American agriculture 1833-1870," *The Journal of Economic History*, Vol. 35, June 1975, pp. 327-52; and in this same *Journal*, Vol. XXII, No. 4, 1962: a special issue on the 100th anniversary of the founding of the US Department of Agriculture. See especially Wayne D. Rasmussen (chief historian of the USDA), "The impact of technological change on American agriculture 1862-1962," pp. 578-91; and Martin Primack, "Land clearing under 19th century techniques," pp. 489-97. A visit to the Smithsonian Institution permanent exhibition on agricultural technology is also highly recommended.

16. US General Accounting Office, *The changing character and structure of American agriculture: an overview* (Report CED-7-178), Washington, D.C., December 1978, p. iii; and John E. Lee, "Agricultural finance: situation and issues," *USDA 1978 Food and Agricultural Outlook Conference*, Proceedings, Washington, D.C., November 1977.

17. USDA, *Alternative Futures for US agriculture: a progress report*, prepared for the Committee on Agriculture and Forestry of the US Senate, by USDA Office of Planning and Evaluation, Washington, D.C., September 1975.

18. On the environmental impact of the high technology system, see Robert van den Bosch, *The Pesticide Conspiracy* (and the preface to it by Paul Ehrlich) Garden City, N.Y., Doubleday, 1978; *Farmers' use of pesticides* (in 1964, 1971, and 1976) USDA Agricultural Economics Reports Nos. 145, 268, 418; David and Marcia Pimentel, *Food, Energy and Society*, Resource and Environmental Science Series, London, Edward Arnold, 1979 (sp. pp. 137-39); Gerald Leach, *Energy and Food Production*, Guilford, Surrey, IPC Science and Technology Press, 1976; Nicole Ball, "Deserts bloom . . . and wither," *Ecologist Quarterly*, Spring 1978.

19. National Academy of Sciences, *Genetic Vulnerability of Major Crops*, Washington, D.C., 1972, p. 1. The best comprehensive report on reduction of seed variety, future germ-plasm resources and the danger of industrial takeover of seeds is Pat R. Mooney, *Seeds of the Earth: a private or public resource?* London, International Coalition for Development Action, a special edition for the UNCSTD Conference, Vienna, 1979.

20. C.F. Erik Eckholm and Frank Record, *The two faces of malnutrition*, Worldwatch Institute Paper No. 9, Washington, D.C., 1976; *Hearings* before the US Senate Select Committee on Nutrition and Human Needs, Washington, D.C., March, April, and May 1973 (in four parts).

21. Nick Kotz, *Hunger in America: The Federal Response*, New York, The Field Foundation, 1979 (quote on p. 23).

22. Susan George, *Feeding the Few: Corporate Control of Food*, Washington, D.C. and Amsterdam, Institute for Policy Studies/Transnational Institute, 1979.

23. Andrew Pearse, "Technology and peasant production: reflections on a global study," *Development and Change*, Vol. 8, 1977. All the UNRISD Studies on the Green Revolution, directed by Pearse, should be consulted on this subject. Definitive conclusions in Andrew Pearse, *Seeds of Plenty, Seeds of Want*, Geneva, Clarendon Press and UNRISD, 1980.

24. Martin Kreisberg, "Miracle seeds and market economies," *Columbia Journal of World Business*, March/April 1969. Kreisberg is now the Coordinator for International Organization Affairs of the Economic Research Service, USDA. His more recent

volume, *International Organizations and Agricultural Development*, USDA, Foreign Agricultural Economic Report No. 131, May 1977, is a compendium showing that donor agency aid goes to implementing the dominant model, e.g., "The IBRD and IDB have put major emphasis on projects . . . to purchase needed production imputs, particularly machinery." p. vii.

25. K.C. Abercrombie, "Agricultural employment in Latin America," *International Labour Organisation Review*, July 1972; and Solon Barraclough and Jacobo Schatan, "Technological change and agricultural development," *Land Economics*, University of Wisconsin, May 1973.

26. Garrison Wilkes, "The world's crop plant germ plasm: an endangered resource," *The Bulletin of the Atomic Scientists*, February 1977; and Mooney, cf. note 19.

27. E. Reuss, "Economic and marketing aspects of post harvest systems in small farmer economics," FAO *Monthly Bulletin of Agricultural Economics and Statistics* (a two-part article), Vol. 25, Nos. 9 and 10, September and October 1976.

28. *Multinational corporations in Brazil and Mexico: structural sources of economic and non-economic power*, Report to the Sub-Committee on Multinational Corporations of the US Senate Committee on Foreign Relations (usually referred to as "The Church Report" from the name of the Committee Chairman), Washington, D.C., August 1975, Appendix A, Table 7.

29. See Susan George, "Nestlé Alimentana, S.A.: The Limits to Public Relations," *Economic and Political Weekly*, Vol. XIII, No. 37, Bombay, 16 September 1978.

30. Details in Charles Medawar, *Insult or Injury?* "An enquiry into the marketing and advertising of British food and drug products in the Third World," London, Social Audit, 1979.

31. Robert Ledogar, *Hungry for Profits: US food and drug multinationals in Latin America*, New York, IDOC, 1976, sp. Ch. 6; and Overseas Private Investment Corporation, *Annual Reports*, 1973 to 1978.

32. Taken directly or calculated from data in USDA, *US Foreign Agricultural Trade Statistical Report*, Calendar Year 1977, Washington, D.C., June 1978.

33. See Maureen McKintosh, "Fruit and Vegetables as an International Commodity," *Food Policy*, November 1977.

34. Cf. Susan George, *Feeding the Few*, op. cit., Part I, and "Le Tiers-Monde face à ses riches clients," *Le Monde Diplomatique*, March 1979.

35. USDA, *Agricultural Outlook*, March 1979, p. 4. Wheat prices in relevant issues of *Business Week*.

36. "Untying aid proves to be a slow process," *Ceres-FAO Magazine*, No. 69, May/June 1979, pp. 4-5 and graph.

37. See *Annual Reports*, P.L. 480 (US food for peace law); and OECD, *Development Cooperation*, Annual Report of the DAC Chairman, 1975, pp. 94-95. This concerns the second and third European Development Fund Commitments. In subsequent DAC reports, the contributions to industrial versus food crops are not broken down, so the situation may have changed since 1975.

38. Further details on the Industry Co-operative Programme in Susan George, *How the Other Half Dies*, Montclair, N.J., Allanheld, Osmun, 1977, Ch. 9.

39. Robert Hirsch, with Boubacar Bah, *Some thoughts on the situation regarding food supplies in the Sahel countries and on the prospects on the horizon for the year 2000*, CILSS and the Club du Sahel, the Nouakchott Colloquy, July 1979, mimeograph. See pp. 20-22, 33, 38.

40. Effects of US food aid in Susan George's *How the Other Half Dies*, op. cit., Ch. 8. A case study on how the cancellation of food aid immediately *improved* the nutritional situation in one country in Thomas Marchione, "Food and nutrition in self-reliant national development: the impact on child nutrition of Jamaican government policy," *Medical Anthropology*, Vol. I, No. 1, Winter 1977. See also Paul Isenman and Hans Singer, "Food Aid, Disincentive Effects and Their Policy Implications," *Economic Development and Cultural Change*, Vol. 25, No. 2, January 1977.

41. "A case for community based oil extraction units in small-farmer oil palm rehabilitation schemes versus the large-scale central milling approach in Nigeria,"

in *Proceedings* of West African Seminar on Agricultural Planning, Zaria, 1974, Ife, Nigerian Institute of Public Administration. The quote is in E. Reusse, op. cit., Part 2, Note 27, and the study is apparently also by Reusse, of FAO, since no other author is cited.

42. World Bank, *Annual Reports*, 1975, p. 55, and 1978, p. 77.

43. E.g., the kind of work being done by UNRISD in the project *Food Systems and Society* could lay the ground for much better-defined development projects, but this kind of research cannot be done in the short "kamikaze" expeditions favored by most lending agencies.

44. For examples, see Khadija Haq, ed., *Equality of Opportunity Within and Among Nations,* Part IV, "Women and Equality of Opportunity," New York and London, Praeger Special Studies, 1977.

45. SAREC (Swedish Agency for Research Co-operation with Developing Countries Bo. Bengtsson, ed., *Rural Development Research: the role of power relations*, Sarec Report R4/1979, p. 38; and Adolfo Mascarenhas, Director of the Bureau of Resources and Land-use Planning (BRALUP), Tanzania, personal communication.

46. Michel Cépède, "Acculturation 'Aristophanique' des communautés rurales et groupes 'Hésiodiques' dans les sociétés industrialisées," paper presented at the World Congress of Sociology, Uppsala, 1978, p. 3.

47. World Bank, *Land Reform*, Rural Development Series, Table 2.2.

48. Prof. Dr. Kurt Egger (and team), *Agro-Technological Alternatives for Agriculture in the Usambara Mountains*, Botanisches Institut der Universitat-Heidelberg, December 1976, mimeograph, p. 22.

49. Ibid., p. 5.

50. E.F.I. Baker and Y. Yusuf, "Mixed cropping research at the Institute for Agricultural Research, Samaru, Nigeria" in *Intercropping in Semi-Arid Areas*, Report on a Symposium, International Development Research Centre, Ottawa, 1976, p. 17 (emphasis added).

51. Mahbub ul Haq, "Toward a Just Society," *International Development Review*, Society for International Development, 1976, No. 4, p. 4.

52. Jere R. Behrman, *International Commodity Agreements: an evaluation of the UNCTAD Integrated Commodity Programme*, Overseas Development Council Monograph No. 9, Washington, D.C., 1977.

Demeter's Dilemma
decolonizing research

This report for the United Nations University (UNU) is the result of a group effort, for which I acted as rapporteur and did the writing. In 1979, Dr. Johan Galtung, who was then directing an ambitious and wide-ranging research project for the UNU called 'Goals, Processes and Indicators of Development', convened a "Food Study Group" in the framework of the GPID project. The Group first met (5-7 February 1979) to produce a paper for a joint seminar of two UNU programs—the World Hunger Program and the Human and Social Development Program (GPID was part of the latter). After this seminar held at MIT in March, the Group reconvened with a number of new people to extend and deepen its initial considerations on research (8-10 July 1979).

The following paper summarizes the FSG's work on these various occasions. Some twenty people were involved in one or both of the Group's working sessions, so it's impossible to indicate here who contributed which elements. But this seems as good a place as any to underline the vital catalytic role of Pierre Spitz, not only in the work of the Food Study Group, but in many of my own writings.

The Group's full membership was: Claude Alvares, Russel Anderson, George Aseniero, Sartaj Aziz, Brita Brandtzaeg, Joseph Collins, Taghi Farvar, Ernest Feder, Louis-François Fleri, Johan Galtung, Susan George, Lim Teck Ghee, Cuautemoc Gonzales P., Papa Kane, Gretchen Klotz, Adolfo Mascarenhas, D.D. Narula, David Pitt, Rahmat Qureshi, Pierre Spitz, Filomina Steady, and Ponna Wignaraja; plus two observers from the UN Research Institute for Social Development, Alemayehu Bessabih and Laurence Wilhelm. The final report is reproduced here (with a few paragraphs from the first paper for the MIT seminar added) and with the kind permission of the United Nations University.

Dimensions and Rationale of the Food Problem

The food problem has many dimensions, but in the context of an economy of consumption it can be visualized as a sliding scale with clinically defined overconsumption at the top and physiological starvation at the bottom, with varying degrees of qualitative and quantitative adequacy and inadequacy between them. Such gradations correspond roughly to socio-economic categories and especially to income levels. The only *serious* food problem in today's world is, however, that of the hunger of millions of people who do not get enough to eat to satisfy their minimum needs.[1]

Hunger exists not only because of the maldistribution of food itself but also because of highly skewed income distribution which precludes the purchase of adequate amounts of food. Maldistribution of income is, in turn, a function of maldistribution of wealth and of a private ownership system which imposes no upper limit on individual or corporate control of the means of production—including those of food production—nor on the amount of wealth which can be accumulated. In contrast, the lower limit, that of zero ownership or even sub-zero ownership (e.g., in the case of chronic indebtedness) is only too clearly defined.

Hunger is also a function of the misappropriation of human and physical resources. Capitalist entrepreneurs are not in the business of providing employment nor of satisfying the needs of society as a whole, but are guided by the profit motive. In capitalist economies, income distribution determines not only consumption but *consumption patterns*. In other words, the system's priorities will encourage the production of foodstuffs and other goods which yield the highest profits and which are therefore geared to satisfying the needs (or the whims) of those who can pay. Such priorities will also, obviously, determine the *use-patterns* of human and physical resources. A perverse resource/use-pattern will correspond to a perverse income/consumption pattern in which market, i.e., monetary, demand will direct the flows of raw materials, including foods, and finished goods.

It is therefore altogether logical that countries in which a high percentage of the population suffers from hunger and malnutrition should often be the same ones that supply traditional or perishable cash crops to affluent purchasers, generally in the northern hemisphere but also to Third World elites. People without purchasing power are placed, ipso facto, outside the market and exert no influence whatever over what it will provide.

Arguments stressing the existence of enough food in the world to furnish each of the planet's inhabitants with a daily diet of over 3,000 calories are striking but may tend to obscure the fact that no country on earth, including the richest, has yet reached the outer limits of what its population (given sufficient income) can consume in terms of *value*, not numerical calories. Wealthy consumers often enjoy regimens of 8,000 to 10,000 calories per day if the large proportion of animal-based products in their diets is calculated in grain-equivalent terms.

It remains to be seen whether a system entirely based on profits and purchasing power will continue to provide some food for the indigent in order to forestall major upheavals which could endanger its overall hegemony. Food aid plays a vital role here, as do free, or subsidized food-distribution schemes. The palliative aspects of food distribution under capitalist conditions will depend on the balance of forces within each particular national community and upon the rank and importance of particular nations in the international system (e.g., the major beneficiaries of food aid). Whatever the level of aid to the destitute, it constitutes neither a permanent nor a structural solution to the persistence of hunger.

Classic Development Strategies and Control over Food Systems

In the past quarter-century, huge transfers of capital and technology have led to the extension of perverse resource-use and resource-enjoyment patterns in the Third World, where the present and probable future food situation must be examined in the context of expanding capitalist control. The tendency of Western development planners and of Third World nationals trained in their methods has been to take a piecemeal approach towards hunger alleviation. Thus, instead of seeing the food problem as a function of a chain, or *system* which begins with inputs (physical as well as intangible, e.g., research and credit), proceeds through food production per se, and continues through the storage, processing, and distribution phases before reaching the final consumer, planners have tended to focus on one or another isolated aspect of the system. The now discredited "Green Revolution" was a strategy concentrating on inputs, the current vogue is for "Post-harvest Technology"; both exhibit a narrow and technocratic approach.

Strategies for particular countries are, furthermore, generally viewed as operating behind closed frontiers, without reference to international market forces or to interventions by agents representing food systems external to the one of the country concerned. To hope that such strategies will succeed—whether they focus on inputs, on increased production, reduction of post-harvest losses, provision of specific nutrients, or on any other segment of the food system chain—is utopian in so far as the central issue of the whole food system has not been confronted: the issue of control.

The question "Who is in control?" may be answered with examples chosen at random from any point along the food system chain; one might begin at the beginning with seeds. Seeds can be selected for maximum yield (given suitable and costly inputs) or for maximum *reliability* under stringent climatic conditions. They may lend themselves to easy self-reproduction or may deteriorate from year to year (e.g., hybrid corn); they may be geared to plants containing maximum nutritional value or, as in some developed countries, to the needs of mechanical harvesters. If *peasants* controlled current research and reproduction of seeds, it is likely that they would ask for, and get, such characteristics as reliability rather than maximum yield, reproductibility rather than deterioration, and high energy/nutritional value. Because seed research and reproduction have been largely under the control of industrialized countries, such characteristics have not generally been sought.

Control over one aspect of the food system implies its extension to others: again, the choice of seeds determines not only the inputs required but also "appropriate" storage and processing techniques.

One highly significant aspect of this issue of control is that exercised by rural oligarchies over poorer peasants: in village after village, a tiny local power elite holds sway over credit, marketing, access to water and other essential services, employment (including that of family members), not to mention the use of the land itself under a variety of more or less extortionate tenancy and sharecropping arrangements. Such power has now been widely recognized; even governments which have done little or nothing to redress the balance pay lip-service to the concept of greater equality and realize that top-heavy power structures act as a "political constraint" on food production.

The Role of Industrialized Countries' Food Systems in the Hunger Problématique

A less widely acknowledged aspect is the increasing degree of control that *developed* country food systems exert over those of the

Third World. The expansion of markets for Green Revolution inputs and other equipment or processes is only a part of the picture. The orientation of Third World agriculture is itself increasingly determined by outsiders who can provide cash markets for various kinds of produce. Many crops formerly produced in the temperate zones for temperate-zone customers are now more cheaply grown in tropical countries. Traditional cash crops have been joined by exports of luxury foods—many of them perishables—and animal foodstuffs.

The penetration of indigenous Third World food systems is largely, though by no means exclusively, carried out by transnational agribusiness corporations. These companies generally no longer wish to exercise direct control over Third World *land*, but gain a stronger hold over *activities*. Operations entailing risk, like farming itself, are left to the LDCs and their peasantries, while more profitable operations such as processing, marketing, and the provision of inputs, credit, or management skills are carried out by foreign corporate interests. The latter have also recently shown a strong interest in providing storage facilities, an area hitherto largely under the control of families, villages, or local authorities.

The Transfer of a Dominant Model

When industrialized countries intervene in the food systems of Third World nations, they are not merely providing separate items and techniques, nor even a "package" of techniques. With the help of their foundations, their universities, their corporations, and their banks, they are transferring a *dominant model*, which, over time, will tend to become unique as it blots out and absorbs the rich variety of peasant practices.

This model originated in the West, particularly in the United States, where prevailing conditions included plentiful land and relatively little labor for food production. It was therefore economically (although no longer ecologically) a rational response to the constraints of a well-defined geographical and social situation. The goal of this model is to obtain the maximum output *per person*, not per unit of land. The conditions which gave rise to this model are wholly untypical of the LDCs, where, on the contrary, the provision of productive employment to large masses of rural people remains a major unmet priority. Because the dominant model contributes to the breakdown of traditional agriculture and to the dispossession of hundreds of thousands of peasants, it can only compound unemployment, while contributing very little, if anything, to increased food production. In any event, incremental production will be even more unfairly distributed by the very fact of unemployment and consequent lack of purchasing power.

Although the promotion of the dominant model can frequently be directly traced to interventions on the part of particular Western governments, international organizations have also played a crucial role. They have at best treated the human and social objectives of development in a rhetorical way and have not allowed this rhetoric to interfere with their basic support for the Western agricultural model in the LDCs. In spite of all declarations to the contrary, they have fostered the emergence and diffusion of high-technology, capital-intensive farming.

Socio-economic Effects of the Dominant Model in the LDCs

The adoption, in whole or in part, of the dominant model by LDC governments, encouraged by international organizations and frequently under pressure from transnational corporation and "aid" partners, has led to a series of disastrous consequences. The gravest among them is the accelerating dissolution of self-provisioning agriculture both as a major element in peasant farming and as a subsistence base of the poorer rural strata—the prime victims of hunger. Some of the other consequences are as follows:

- Relations of production and exchange, formerly oriented more directly to the maintenance of family livelihoods, become commercialized.

- Competition between peasants and entrepreneurial farms for the use of good quality land increases in direct response to higher demand for both food and export crops.

- The environment suffers as increasing numbers of families try to extract a livelihood from land that is diminishing in area and deteriorating in quality because of the over-use and improper husbandry they are obliged to practice for immediate survival.

- Agricultural "modernization" strikes women particularly hard. They are among the first to be eliminated when commercialized farming overtakes self-provisioning, as the consecutive Indian censuses of 1961 and 1971 clearly illustrate. During that decade, two-thirds of all female cultivators ceased activity, while the number of female agricultural laborers increased by 50 percent.

- Food "imperialism" accompanies the introduction of the dominant model. The "baby-foods scandal" provides a flagrant example, but other foods have received less attention. Some, like bread or soft drinks, may gain great prestige. Although the dominant model may promote commercial pseudo-variety (as in US-style supermarkets), true cultural variety inherent in the production, preparation, and consumption of a broad spectrum of foods is markedly declining. This decline is accompanied by the deterioration of nutritional levels. Commercial promotion of Western processed foods downgrades not only local diets per se but also the symbolic value of traditional foods perceived, by comparison, as culturally inferior. Third World elites may take the lead in such consumption and are then imitated by their less privileged compatriots.

- Food aid plays a vital role in the introduction of new dietary habits. It can also create a bias towards foreign solutions of local problems: whereas nutritionists in Mysore State had developed suitable high protein foods from local raw materials, their formula was rejected in favor of the corn-soya-milk blend provided by the US PL 480 Food Aid Program.

- Countries whose "export-led" agricultural strategies cause them to emphasize the supply of foreign markets, and to forsake their peasantries attempting to produce food for local consumption, grow increasingly dependent on massive cereal imports, tying them both economically and politically to privileged suppliers, more often than not the United States.

- Outside interventions and transfers of technology tend to reproduce the high-capital, low-labor-intensive characteristics of industrialized countries' food systems. This necessarily increases the *cost* of food, which must remunerate invested capital (e.g., centralized storage adds an estimated 20 percent to the cost of grains sold in LDCs, according to an FAO expert). This, of course, places food beyond the reach of poor consumers and contributes to eliminating peasants who cannot compete in wholly mercantilized food systems.

The Rapid Decline of Self-Provisioning

However deleterious these consequences of the introduction of the dominant model (the above list is far from complete) it must be stressed that the most serious among them is the marked decline of self-provisioning agriculture.

The drama of this process of decay lies in the fact that the "umbilical" attachment of people to the land at the level of the family or kin-group is, with all its insecurities and natural hazards, the food system that has maintained humankind during most of its history. In the market-oriented developing countries, trends are encouraged that inevitably confirm or accelerate the decline of self-provisioning before other forms of economic activity are able to offer alternative means of livelihood to the displaced peasantry. As a consequence, marginalization and proletarianization are proceeding inexorably in Asia, Africa, and Latin America, though at differing speeds and in different ways.

The full significance of this transformation is not entirely comprehended, but it seems to imply deterioration in the nourishment of the already poor as they are obliged to purchase food in unfavourable conditions from the market; massive migration to urban centres and a much higher level of conflict, disorder and repression. The removal of productive assets from women through new forms of division of labour in agricultural production may often result in a serious reduction of food provided to rural families.[2]

The actual producers of food—the overwhelmingly rural majorities of the Third World—are being progressively divested of their control over what they shall produce, by what methods, and of the resulting harvest. Imitation of the Western high-technology model and continued subservience to the needs of outside food systems cannot be expected to eliminate hunger—only to make it worse. The relevant questions in the "hunger problématique" have become: "Who controls the surplus?" "Who has the power to define what constitutes the 'surplus' at the expense of the starving and malnourished?"

Science, Scientists, and the Hunger Problem[3]

The relationship between "science" and "development" is not a transparent one. A close and critical examination of this relationship may be itself a contribution to development and, ultimately, to science as well. Most Western scientists would see the following statements as unproblematic:

- Science is/should be "value-free," "objective."
- The task of science is to discover *laws*.
- These laws should be as general as possible.
- The scientist (at least in his professional capacity) is a competent expert, tolerant, open-minded, and politically neutral.

The label "value-free" may hide a host of hidden values and assumptions of which the researcher may be unaware (although they may be obvious to others and surface in dialogue or confrontation). Scientific laws are conceived as reflecting a basically *unchanging* empirical reality. And in the notion of working towards "general" laws, there is a clear norm of universalism. Behind laws lie *paradigms*, or generally accepted fundamental beliefs about phenomena, describing their nature but also defining the kinds of new investigations that can be undertaken *without challenging the basic hypotheses*.

The preceding set of propositions might be contrasted with a concept of science which would not hide values and assumptions but try to make them explicit and subject to challenge and exploration. Such a science would be concerned not only with *seeking* invariances but also with *breaking* them; it would seek fewer universals and more insights relevant to the particularities of specific points in space and time. (Catastrophe theory is concerned with just such questions and is beginning to provide the mathematical structures for a science far more attuned to the qualitative and the discontinuous than to the quantifiable and the regular. It also stresses the irreversibility of certain phenomena and the impossibility of predicting them.)

The fundamental debate about Western science in general, and the positivist orientation in particular, has clear relevance for the discussion of any specific science, especially when the historical and socio-economic origins of these branches of knowledge are examined.

Most science is goal-oriented, and geared either to production or to social control. Science began to serve the now-dominant economic system around the seventeenth century, but since the nineteenth century this relationship has become more explicit. The maritime character of the British Empire was not without influence on the development of meteorology and naval astronomy; nor was the rational exploitation of colonial possessions unrelated to the establishment of agronomy, minerology, and tropical medicine as separate branches of knowledge. It is not surprising that the earliest agricultural research focused on cash crops to the exclusion of African or Asian food crops. Nutrition studies, as first undertaken in Europe, were designed to determine the minimum standards necessary for assuring the reproduction of the industrial labor force (particularly miners).

Present-day scientists may agree with Mao Zedong that science is the crystallization of knowledge developed through humankind's struggle for production, but it is also their duty to ask, "Production for whom?" If science is to become relevant to the real needs of the Third World and to have any favorable impact on human and social development, it must undertake a fundamental re-examination of its goals and its methods.

What then are some of the issues and obstacles that must be faced by individuals and institutions seeking to help transform the hunger problématique through the use of the instruments of scholarship? We shall specifically refer here to "research," but our remarks almost invariably apply to other activities carried out by intellectuals, like education and training.

New Slogans versus Old Realities

There seems now to be near-universal recognition, at least at the rhetorical level, that "growth models" and once-popular "technological fixes" have not worked. Policies favoring capital-intensive, import-substitution industrial development have led to neglect of agriculture as a whole, and, within the agricultural sector, the wealthiest and most "progressive" producers have received attention at the expense of small peasants and landless laborers. As we have stressed, these groups have become increasingly unable to produce enough or to buy enough food to meet their minimum needs. Such statements may now be regarded as truisms, but this does not mean that development agents and agencies are acting on their implications.

The proven ineffectiveness of liberal solutions for the pressing problems of the Third World has not even been accompanied by a genuine conceptual change of heart. Old slogans ("GNP growth," "trickle down," "take-off," etc.) wear out and are discarded, yet their replacements look suspiciously similar behind new facades. Concepts which may have been innovative when formulated by Third World leaders are deradicalized by the development establishment, or this establishment simply forges its own new "appropriate terminology." Two *potentially* radical concepts currently undergoing this watering-down process are the New International Economic Order and Basic Needs.[4]

So long as this establishment maintains the conceptual initiative and is able to impose its own terms of reference, it will hold an important tool for entrenching the status quo. Progressive scholars must attempt to regain the initiative in this area.

Technical Solutions versus Politics

Although one now sees numerous references to the "political will necessary" for carrying out the bland recommendations of international conferences, in practice development expertise generally confines itself to technical questions supposedly amenable to technical solutions. The all-important political dimensions in any real development (which always implies gains for some and losses for others) is left out.

The "development intelligentsia" also treads carefully even where *technical* issues are concerned, avoiding examination of the social and political context in which they are placed. In designing projects, implementing scientific discoveries (e.g., Green Revolution seed varieties) or planning changes in technology, it usually ignores the following postulates which ought to be obvious to any neutral observer:

1. A project (scientific discovery, technological innovation, etc.) benefiting the least favored classes will not be acceptable to the dominant classes unless their interests are also substantially served.
2. A project ... which benefits *only* the poor will be ignored, sabotaged, or otherwise suppressed by the powerful insofar as possible.
3. A project ... which serves the interests of the dominant classes while doing positive harm to the poor may still be put into practice and if necessary maintained by violence so long as no basic change in the balance of political and social forces takes place.[5]

Development experts design programs they claim will "reach" the poor while offering no guarantees to that effect. The implementation of projects in which the poor stand to benefit may succeed so long as the area is saturated with capital and so long as these projects are administered over small areas by dedicated personnel having no particular interests to defend. It is, however, unrealistic to suppose that beyond the pilot stage, market forces will not intervene and that the wealthier and more powerful elements of society will not appropriate whatever technical and financial benefits the project was designed to create.

Systemic Adjustments versus Structural Change

Most research presently carried out by development agencies is concerned with "face-lifting" operations, not structural change, and starts from the premise that the present world system, given a few compromises, can be made to work for everyone, as it is claimed to have worked for everyone in the now-developed countries.

The Food Study Group does not believe systemic adjustments (e.g., the inclusion of more people in Green Revolution-type strategies), even if they occur, will change the status of the masses of hungry people more than marginally. Thus we cannot advocate research basically committed to "tinkering" with present structures. This is a waste of time if one's goals are really to benefit those who presently lack all control over the circumstances of their lives. Aside from what we consider the false premises and the self-serving nature of such scholarship, we might also point out that those seeking systemic adjustments rarely if ever consult the poor and powerless people their research is nominally designed to serve. Top-down research design and project implementation is still the rule.

We also take note that successful systemic adjustments in the past (successful, that is, in staving off acute social conflict) have to a large degree created conditions that make improvement in the status of the poorest members of society virtually impossible. One example submitted to the Group (by D.D. Narula) is that of the very limited land reform in India, which nonetheless extended rural control from 1 to 2 percent of the landholders to 18 to 19 percent today. It will be far more difficult to dislodge this recently created class than the previous feudal one without profound and painful social change.

Much research sponsored by major donors is also directed toward helping people *to make do with less* rather than aiding them to obtain more. Efforts are directed to "getting the most from" an environment already depleted by the greed of national or international interests which have reduced the quantity and quality of resources available to the poor. Little work is devoted to strategies for regaining even those rights that theoretically belong to the most deprived, much less for demanding new ones.

How should one approach research basically concerned with such stop-gaps? There are delicate moral problems involved here: one cannot avoid the problems of immediate survival facing the poor *today*, nor discount the possibility of perhaps saving a few lives through palliative measures that may help the powerless temporarily and in limited ways. Thus we would not state categorically that one should not engage in alleviating, wherever possible, the miserable conditions of the hungry. But this sort of work is, like it or not, on the level of "systems tinkering" and basically accepts the status quo. It should not therefore be a priority for those who hope to do relevant work against the mainstream.

Conflict with the Dominant Research Establishment

As in other areas of human affairs, the area of research is a terrain for conflict—at least when anything of importance is at stake. When there is general agreement on what constitutes the proper province of scholarly objectives and activities, one may assume that those who have an interest in maintaining the existing balance of power do not feel themselves threatened. Progressive scholars should thus welcome conflict as an admission that their work is doing powerless people some good, or might aid them in the future. This is a serious responsibility and places upon such researchers the burden of being more rigorous than their detractors and opponents while at the same time avowing and defending their "value-loaded" approach.

The most immediate conflicts for progressive intellectuals and institutions will occur with the dominant research establishment which will quite naturally seek to maintain and increase its control over scholars and scholarship.

This establishment has a number of ways of ensuring its hegemony. One of the simplest and most effective, as some Third World Food Study Group members have brought out, is merely to occupy the terrain. Western foundations, universities, aid agencies, etc., appear in force in country X and immediately enlist the cooperation of all, or nearly all, the available scientific manpower, expertise, laboratories, and institutions available. In most Third World countries, indigenous scientific capacity is underfunded to begin with, so it is materially feasible to put whatever capacity exists to work on spurious projects—or even on projects that quite candidly serve the needs of donor countries (as is the case with US "Food for Peace" counterpart funds spent on agricultural or "market development" research carried out in aid-recipient countries by indigenous scientists).

Any project proposed independently and designed to be of real assistance to the poorest and least influential groups, or one which might lead to a change in existing social relations, is, in effect, placed in direct competition with handsomely funded programs which generally appeal to governments as much as they do to large and powerful donors. As one of our members says, speaking of the obstacles encountered in trying to start a small project targeted to the poorest people in a country heavily populated by development experts, "I found the patterns of allocation of resources and grants strongly biased towards these well-established and dominant research institutions whose main objective seems to be confined to their own reproduction and development. In this respect the role of international agencies was determinant." If by some freak occurrence an innovative project does get underway, according to this same participant, "it becomes the focus of attention of international donors and observers visiting the country, receives a lot of publicity and diverts attention from the real (overall development prospects) in that country." Such innovations, if they cease to be invisible to planners, take on an alibi status; in both cases they can be made to serve the system's needs. It is unwise for a local scientist to protest such an orientation of the scientific capacity of his country: "The only two scientists who contested the way in which research was undertaken in the major . . . institution were fired from their assignments."

Another member points out that a position in the international research establishment is richly rewarded—the highest priority for Third World intellectuals apparently being at present expert status with the World Bank. This is also why they strive to obtain diplomas from prestigious Western institutions—these are much more highly rewarded than degrees from Third World universities.

A third member analyzes the social realities of research carried out in underdeveloped countries as follows.

Most funds for research come from outside the country (from industrialized-country sources) so it is understandable that the objectives, the methodologies, and the terms of reference also be dictated from the outside. Some work by PhD candidates is done for established professors with their own theories to defend. Younger scholars must conform to the professors' guidelines if they want to find a job in academia later on. Scholarship may also serve to support the foregone conclusions of decision-makers or of the international development-planners who so frequently dictate the choices of national planners.

Scholars are virtually told what their findings are expected to be. Such work obtains recognition for the intellectual in government and/or academic circles, whereas independent, progressive researchers are rarely promoted. It is no wonder that their number is infinitesimally small compared to the numbers of "yes men" (and "yes women"). The near-total irrelevance of most social science curricula to the value systems, perspectives, or historical evolution of Third World peoples has also been stressed by Food Study Group members.

The Dominant Research Model: Prestige without Accountability

We have attempted to show how the dominant Western agricultural model is being propagated in the Third World with harmful consequences. (The same could be said for other areas—e.g., health care, industrial development under the aegis of transnational corporations, etc.) That there is also a dominant model in research, accepted and admired by most Third World intellectuals and seen as prestigious by their governments, cannot be overstressed.

This prestige is not fortuitous. As Pierre Spitz points out, the dominant research establishment is actually engaged in two kinds of work. The first is empirical and operational and hews very close to reality because it is concerned with a more efficient manipulation and management of that reality. The audience for which it is prepared is a limited one; much of this work is confidential and restricted to the commissioning agency. It *must*, in fact, be largely confidential *because* of its adherence to reality, because most reality *is* oppression.

The second kind of work is more closely related to ensuring this model's dominance through the production and dissemination of an ideology destined for the broadest possible audience, spread by a variety of media and institutions, including universities. The practitioners of the first kind of scholarship should have no difficulty identifying the interests they are serving: they share these interests to the degree they are rewarded by them. Scholars in the second group may not always understand the role they are playing. If so, they are themselves victims of the dominant ideology—naive but not dishonest; if not, then cynical or motivated by gain. Both kinds of work may, of course, be done at different times by the same persons.

Almost all research is geared either to production or to social control and is carried out for institutions (e.g., transnational corporations, leading foundations, lending agencies like the World Bank) which exercise power without any mitigating accountability. "Production" in this context means production of goods and services which are wanted and can be paid for by consumers with purchasing power. This aim automatically precludes research and development addressed to satisfying the needs of those who live in poverty. The bodies which impose these goals on present research are answerable to no one—except a hand-picked board—and the Food Study Group considers it fruitless to ask, or to expect, them to change their aims. They are not to be persuaded, but rather confronted and exposed.

That members of the power structures are willing to devote substantial resources to research indicates that the latter is not a luxury good but an important input to control: it helps to strengthen the power of those who exercise it while simultaneously contributing to thickening the ideological smokescreen behind which this power is exercised.

Some Elements of a Progressive Approach to Research

Research on Research

One immediately necessary task for progressive scholarship is to confront the dominant research establishment on its own ground. The sheer weight of resources devoted to spurious or irrelevant projects in the Third World ensures that the enormous body of work turned out will have a wide influence. (One may, for example, recall the success of the "overpopulation-is-the-cause-of-hunger" school.) The Food Study Group's refusal to condone or participate in this kind of scholarship thus carries an important corollary: we see it as one obligation of intellectuals to carry out "research on research" if they hope to undermine the dominant model's influence and compete for its audience in both developed and underdeveloped countries. It is important to examine *what* establishment research covers and *why* particular projects (and, of course, particular countries) are of special interest to bilateral and multilateral funders at particular times. It should be a relatively easy task to ascertain which social groups stand to benefit from the choice of certain projects over others.

Studying the Powerful

Related to this target (examining power by examining its uses of the instruments of scholarship) is the importance of studying the dominant social and political forces both spatially and temporally. The Food Study Group believes that the reasons for poverty and hunger are not to be found mainly *within* the class of the poor and hungry but in their *relationships* with the rest of society (from the local to the national to the international level). The most important focus for research on poverty, which itself causes hunger, can be summarized in the single word "power": power as it is expressed in social classes and through the institutions that serve them at every level.

In *The Crisis of Democracy* the Trilateral Commission castigated "value-oriented intellectuals" who "devote themselves to the derogation of leadership, the challenging of authority and the unmasking and delegitimisation of established institutions" including those responsible for "the indoctrination of the young."[6]

We would assert that intellectuals should not only be value-oriented but indeed devote themselves to just those tasks decried by the Trilateral Commission. This can be achieved in different ways at different levels.

As Pierre Spitz again notes, there is a hierarchy in research (which is not to imply that one kind has more intrinsic *worth* than another): (1) factual or empirical work, in which the researcher's values naturally determine the topics pursued and the facts sought; (2) research designed to verify a hypothesis clearly defined at the outset and in which facts serve this aim; (3) epistemological research concerned with the very concepts and paradigms that underlie research and the tools it uses. At each of these levels, dichotomies (and conflicts) between the dominant and the dominated classes are, or should be, apparent. One of the tasks of research is to unmask the interests involved at every level—interests which will also determine the clientele for, and the uses made of, research. We do not wish to give the impression that research can be separated from its applications, particularly from its role in the creation of a dominant ideology and its dissemination through the mass media or educational and training institutions.

Multidisciplinary Studies

There has been a general recognition, at least in the progressive scholarly community, that single-discipline research for rural

61.

development is not the road to success. Although single-discipline work still prevails in the far greater part of scholarly output, there are numerous signs that a multidisciplinary approach is becoming fashionable. This itself will not constitute a panacea. If the disciplines, whatever their nature and number, still revolve around the old paradigms and tackle the wrong problems (or the right problems in the wrong ways) they might easily do more harm than the previously more limited approach. Multidisciplinary work could, however, become an important instrument if it were to take on the issue of power as it expresses itself at the global, regional/national, and local levels.

Creating and Using New Stocks of Knowledge and Innovative Methodologies

Beneath the "growth model" that dominated development thinking for so many fruitless years lay the assumption that there was a unique stock of knowledge (science and technology), that this was the exclusive preserve of the industrialized countries, and that it needed to be transferred along with capital if Third World nations were ever to "bridge the gap." But a concept of *human* development cannot mean "Western" or "elitist." Does anyone really believe that insight is so asymmetrically distributed that billions of men and women deeply engaged in food production, preparation, distribution, and consumption know nothing at all, whereas a few selected researchers (nutritionists, social scientists, agronomists, et al.) know everything? Thus stated, most would agree that there must exist huge stocks of knowledge beyond the confines of "official" science and technology, but that they have gone largely uncollected, untapped, and unutilized. There may be, in fact, four separate stocks of knowledge, of which two are as yet largely uncreated:

1. Western, positivist, mechanistic science and technology;
2. traditional, empirical, operational stocks of knowledge, stored by peasants and closely adapted to survival skills within the constraints of a wide variety of environments;
3. knowledge which might come from interaction between (1) and (2), if only self-satisfied "experts" can be persuaded to listen and learn, and peasants, so long disdained, can be persuaded they have something to teach;
4. knowledge which might come from the significant demand in many *developed* countries for a simpler, more humane life-style.

New nature/human/technology "mixes" are needed, including many that have not been imagined yet, but which might be part of that

"Third Science" stemming from a real dialogue between North and South, peasants and experts. This would necessarily imply sharing decision-making power as well as knowledge; as mass consciousness increased, elites would find their power diminishing.[7]

Methodologies of the social sciences in particular (but also of nutrition) developed during the late nineteenth and early twentieth centuries in an urban, industrial, masculine, Western context. They are thus more apt to be good at defining—and answering—questions posed by urban, industrial, masculine Western societies. Research has not only treated people like objects, but has suffered from environment-blindness, sex-blindness, and age-blindness. Nutritional science, for example, knows relatively little about traditional mixes and sequences of foods making maximum of the environment. When it does take an interest in such matters, it is often to discover that Western inroads are destroying dietary practices with a sound scientific basis (e.g., food combinations ensuring optimum balance of amino acids). The invisibility of women in most development-planning can only be corrected when women themselves take an active part in the planning process. Something is known about infants and children under five (unfortunately, mortality statistics form a large part of this knowledge) but very little work has been done on old people. Third World people may have lower life expectancies, but they also age more quickly. In fragile food systems, children and old people suffer disproportionately; just as they, along with women, are the first to be eliminated from productive work when control shifts from local communities to outside forces.

People have their own ways of stocking information, but these are rarely the ways that figure on social scientists' questionnaires. If peasants are asked, for example, how large a yield they produced, or how much they spent on cloth last year, or even how large their plot of ground is, they may have difficulty answering, but this does not mean they are ignorant. Their measurement and information system merely uses other criteria: e.g., the "quantity price," or amount that can be bought with one unit of currency at different times of the year; or the "commodity basket" of purchases that are approximately the same every week or month; or the number of months they and their families were able to live off their own harvest without having recourse to purchased food. Questions asked inside the peoples' terms of reference will receive useful answers.

Surveyors who have rarely ever been hungry themselves can perhaps not be expected to realize immediately that *annual* data about food intake would seem strange indeed to peasants and their families whose problem is survival tomorrow, next week, and next month, especially during the lean season. Surveys could, however, very usefully look at fluctuations rather than averages for various socio-economic groups. A survey of a village one month before and one month after harvest would give entirely different results.[8] This means that projects would have to last longer and that the "people's methodology" would have to be adopted in order to learn something worth knowing.

The "Objects" of Research Must Become Its Subjects

Those for whom progressive research is purportedly being done—the poor and hungry—must be consulted about their needs and helped by the researcher to define those needs. We believe that the worst-off know very well why they are poor, at least on the immediate local level, and that this knowledge represents one starting point for improving their status. This can only come about through various forms of organization in which the researcher should take as active a role as is warranted by the expressed desire of the community in question. We are not sure there are any serious thinkers who still believe in scholarly neutrality, but, if so, we would like to paraphrase Orwell and point out that "all researchers are neutral, but they are more neutral towards some social groups than towards others."

It is here that the problem of the *accountability* of the researcher should be posed. Intellectuals working at the "micro" or community level should be accountable to that community, and the worth of their work determined by the degree of relevance to its felt needs. (Scholars concerned with "macro" level issues might well be judged, on the other hand, by the degree of controversy and confrontation their work gives rise to.)

Real development is incompatible with methodologies which envisage only the collection of data by an "objective, impartial" scholar using a pre-designed survey questionnaire. There must also exist a commitment on the researcher's part actively to foster social change in the desirable direction. The intellectual must feel a sense of identity with the situation and, perhaps most difficult, must accept to be changed by the research process; as of course the *researched* will also change if there has been real interaction. "Participatory" or "dialogic" research emphasizes the holistic approach, i.e., for food problems the researcher would enter into a dialogue with the people about life in the community as a whole, because food, nutrition, health, etc., are not viewed separately but as parts of life. The people's identification of the problem, their assessment of the obstacles to solving it, and their proposals for doing so in spite of the obstacles should form the total process leading to meaningful action. Interaction between "expert" and people should upgrade traditional knowledge as well as create new knowledge to be integrated into community practice.

The important point is that any research project is *itself a part of the power structure*; a progressive project should thus be concerned either with (1) denouncing with factual proof present power arrangements and their harmful effects on the poor—or at least showing the gap between rhetoric and reality in the way power speaks about itself (the "discourse") or (2) strengthening the capacity of the poor to organize and free themselves from oppression. It is likely that most projects would not be able fully to combine these two aspects, and that one person would not be able to do both kinds of work, but both are important. An unresolved problem is how to establish fruitful collaboration and continuing contact between scholars engaged in type (1) or (2) so that their work becomes mutually reinforcing. A progressive research/educational institution could play a very important role in facilitating and maintaining such contacts. It might be particularly helpful to groups in the Third World to be able to make their needs known to scholars in the developed countries where access to documentation on the power centers is easier.

Research Outside the Dominant Food-System Model

We have attempted to make clear the concept of a food system and to suggest that there are large systems, or cycles, spanning countries, continents, or the whole globe which are gaining in importance; while small food cycles—self-provisioning on a family, community, or regional level—are declining. This is perhaps an inexorable and irreversible movement; we cannot say. We believe, however, that it is the duty of the researcher and the development-planner to protect, to strengthen, and to enhance the smaller cycles in all possible ways; to resist the encroachment of the large ones which are leading to increased hunger in the world.

It is particularly urgent that scientific research outside the dominant agricultural model be undertaken without delay. Without wishing to appear apocalyptic, we would still like to point out that a new world food crisis may be looming which could make the crisis of 1972-74 seem pale by comparison. The World Food Conference of 1974 predicted that the developing countries would be importing around 85 million tons of food in 1985. By 1978-79, the figure had already gone beyond 70 million tons (as compared to 50 million tons in 1976-77). After several years of abundance in the late 1970s, the stocks of the major grain exporters (particularly the United States) were being intentionally drawn down with the result that a bushel of US wheat which sold for $3.12 in late August of 1978 is worth $4.43 at this writing (November 1979), and had gone as high as $4.60 in July before the first new harvests came in. The food dependency of most importing countries is increasing, not declining, and the failure of governments to conclude a new International Wheat Agreement in February 1979 is another ominous sign. Most observers believe that developed countries will continue to devote even greater amounts of grain to feeding animals in their own countries, thus further limiting available supplies.

The equilibrium of international food markets, with their reliance on the US and to a lesser extent a handful of smaller exporters such as Canada, is so precarious that any relatively minor shock—climatic or commercial—could set off a disproportionate market reaction for which the Third World would have to pay. Outsized purchases by a major importer such as the Soviet Union or China; blight, or failure of the monsoon in Asia; a drop in US production; any or all could trigger an uncontrollable upward spiral in prices as speculation took hold. Food aid cannot be expected to palliate such conditions: the historical record shows that aid decreases as commercial purchases increase in the context of tight markets.

Only those countries deemed politically vital would continue to receive a significant supply of food aid in a period of scarcity. To these disquieting factors must be added the increasing reliance of Third World food systems, imitating the dominant system, on energy-dependent inputs like fuels, fertilizers, and other petroleum-based chemicals. This comes at a time when even increased OPEC-country aid cannot compensate for their mounting costs, particularly since Western transnational corporations largely control the marketing of these products.

Many Third World governments seem to be living in a sort of fool's paradise, lulled by several years of good weather and resultant good harvests—and perhaps by a belief in the benevolence of their traditional aid partners and suppliers of major food grains. The present food system, with its reliance on high-energy, high-technology inputs, is growing more vulnerable daily, to the point that it is not unrealistic to speak of an eventual systemic breakdown.

If systems breakdowns do occur (and, to many of us, this outcome appears to be only a matter of time) then we will long for the days when a different kind of complexity—biological, not industrial—made our farming systems more resilient and disaster-resistent.[9]

The higher the level of complex industrial technology in a given system, the more fragile and less capable of withstanding crisis it becomes. From this point of view, the systems in the industrialized countries are the most exposed to breakdown, whereas in the Third World there is still time to preserve and to improve the traditional farming practices which have provided the basis for human survival through several millennia. This, however, with rare exceptions is not being done.

On the contrary—not surprising given the intellectual prestige and financial backing of the dominant model in both agriculture and research—most resources are being devoted to fine-tuning the dominant model itself to fit a greater variety of local conditions. Adolfo Mascarenhas reports, for example, that in Tanzania there is an area where peasants are capable of identifying and cultivating 24 different varieties of rice. Yet there is no Tanzanian (much less outside) research team monitoring their practices with the aim of understanding them in a more codifiable and "scientific" way. On the other hand, research grants are being awarded for work on imported varieties of hybrid rice.

One encouraging example of research outside the dominant agronomic model which has come to our attention is the work being done by a team at Heidelberg University. This group takes an "archaeological" approach to land-use practices of traditional farmers (e.g., the Kikuyu farmers in the Kilimanjaro region of Kenya) in order to understand the functional principles involved. The Kikuyu system is multi-faceted, and includes various tree crops, bushes, standing crops, and "weeds" (which play a positive protective role); a system characterized by high species diversity, stability, and complexity able to withstand the particular hazards of the local environment. The Kikuyu peasants exhibit great skill in arranging the species so that they interact with one another; they have also perfected anti-erosion and waste-using techniques demonstrating a high level of scientific sophistication. Some of the lessons learned in Kenya have subsequently been used by this Heidelberg team in designing a minimum-physical-inputs system for farm improvement in Rwanda. They have also developed a similar approach in Mexico, using Mayan cultivation practices as a starting point.

In the context of a traditional system, generally a very efficient user of energy, it is entirely possible to integrate technological elements from outside the original system at fairly low cost. This can be desirable so long as it is the *farmers themselves* who determine what new technologies are opportune and so long as they retain control over the system as a whole. Thus we are not advocating a museum-conservation approach to traditional systems, however good, nor a goal of simply replicating them, but rather a creative blending of local expertise with Western scientific knowledge.

Or, as the UN Research Institute for Social Development has put it,

> We do not suggest . . . that modern production techniques should be rejected as such or that self-provisioning agriculture must be maintained or restored as a necessary basis for food systems and rural

livelihood. What is suggested, however, is that the transition to higher levels of technology, increased capitalization and further economies of scale can only be achieved by means of firm and carefully prepared policies and programmes with the active participation of the different social groups concerned, and that much of the knowledge essential to the adequate preparation and execution of such policies is not available. In addition, the political will for such programmes and policies can hardly be expected to appear spontaneously in social structures that provide poor peasant groups with little power or influence. The worst danger is the precipitate uprooting and marginalization of rural majorities and nomadic fringe groups before alternative sources of livelihood are available to them.

Research beyond the confines of the dominant agricultural model could reduce such dangers to the degree that it strengthened traditional food systems, thus making the communities practicing them more resistant to outside pressures. The knowledge that lies behind traditional systems is not always readily accessible to outsiders and can only be acquired through cooperation with peasant practitioners—easier said than done, especially for Westerners.

The Food Study Group has concluded that a major responsibility incumbent on institutions consciously directing their work against mainstream research and aspiring to help solve the food/hunger problem is to support "creative dissidents," who should find an important place in future research.

Summary and Recommendations

1. Research should be undertaken on the impact of *global* power structures at national and local levels in underdeveloped countries. Politics of particular actors (e.g., transnational corporations, multilateral agencies, industrialized states, etc.) should be examined to ascertain their effects on food/hunger in the Third World.

2. Research at the *national* level should include an action/participatory component and should incorporate findings from the global level. The object of such work should not merely be to collect data but to initiate social change. It should also aim at upgrading and conserving traditional farming systems in each country.

3. Research is also required at the *epistemological* level, and would include "research on research," examination of paradigms, creation of new knowledge stocks and methodologies; the placing of research and development systems in historical perspective. The creative dissidents span all these elements and contribute to their evolution. This epistemological component is not some sort of "philosophical window-dressing" but a vital contribution to regaining what we

have called the "conceptual initiative." Until the terms of reference can be changed, research and development programs will remain in the usual technocratic ruts.

4. The ultimate *goal* of all this work should be to educate, train, sensitize and remold national elites and to raise mass consciousness for social change. Assuming governments and other elites *want* to contribute to solving the food/hunger problem, they will need not only data on the interests which presently prevent this, but also a decolonized conceptual approach that relativizes and delegitimizes the dominant model(s) in any number of disciplines. Such a decolonized approach should be transmitted through educational and training institutions which should help people to recapture and liberate their own creativity—as individuals and as nations. Although this report has concentrated more on the theoretical elements of a hunger problématique, research critique, and proposals for change, we believe that most of our observations apply to education and training as well. In other words, there are dominant models in curricula, pedagogical methods, etc.; these models are instituted and maintained by particular classes whose interests they serve; there are also creative dissidents working outside these models who need support. One form of support is the provision of alternative curricular tools. Participatory research is a form of education which raises mass consciousness, just as the exposure of present repressive power structures is one necessary step toward freeing creativity.

Conclusion

Ideally, people should be in a position to make a *choice* as to the kind of food/agricultural system they prefer and to carry it out based *on their own design*, but we are very far away from that goal. The Food Study Group is aware that all its recommendations run counter to currently observable trends: more centralized state bureaucracies, growing power of transnational corporate capitalism, etc. Greater popular control over food-producing resources and food itself seems, however, the only viable long-term strategy against hunger. Useful research will foster this strategy and not only will try to help the now-powerless to formulate what they want and need, but will also attempt to provide them with useful information about the power structures that work against them so that they may frame more realistic strategies.

It is obvious that these strategies, like those of any real human and social development, will involve political conflict; this cannot be avoided. We are not, however, engaged in waiting for the revolution, which has little more to recommend it than waiting for the afterlife.

We do believe that with the cooperation of men and women of goodwill everywhere—North or South, intellectuals or peasants—it is possible to build up countervailing powers, to work for slow revolution, to discover available political spaces and to create new ones within which it is possible to struggle against the economic and class interests which have no scruples about eliminating millions of people. As John Berger has written,

> The peasantry as a class is the oldest in existence. It has shown remarkable powers of survival—powers which have puzzled and confused most administrators and theorists. In fact . . . the essential character of the peasantry . . . despite all the important differences of climate, religion, economic and social history . . . actually derives from its being a class of survivors. It is often said that the majority of people in the world today are still peasants. Yet this fact masks a more significant one. For the first time ever, it is possible that the class of survivors may not survive.[10]

We see it as the task of intellectuals to recognize our debt to this class of survivors, our common interest not only that they endure but that they prosper. We must be prepared to move forward with them; to do so, we must be prepared to abandon our comfortable hypotheses, our scientific certainties, our favorite wisdoms—including, perhaps, those set forth in this paper.

Notes

1. On this and other questions in this report, see "Toward a World without Hunger: Progress and Prospects for Completing the Unfinished Agenda of the World Food Conference," a report by the Executive Director of the World Food Council, WFC/1979/3, 23 March 1979; E.g., "To get additional food into the diets of those [hundreds of millions who are chronically hungry] involves much more than increasing food production. . . . Greater production does not ensure that the increased food available will reach large numbers of hungry and malnourished people, nor can selective programmes for nutrition intervention—useful as they are—meet the needs of large malnourished populations afflicted by a shortage of food energy or calories. . . . Basically, the main obstacle to meeting the nutritional needs of large populations is one of poverty or lack of 'effective demand.' . . . [Solutions] must be sought in development policies which increase employment for the rural landless and the urban poor and stimulate increased production by small subsistence farmers." Paras. 121, 123.
2. These two paragraphs are taken from the United Nations Research Institute for Social Development's project report *Food Systems and Society* with whose analysis the FSG is in full agreement. The Group wishes to draw particular attention to this study: UNRISD/78/C.14/Rev. 1 (quote from p. 21).
3. Questions discussed in this section are more fully treated in the Food Study Group's *Issues Paper* (Susan George, Rapporteur): HSDRGPID-2/UNUP-54, United Nations University, 1979.
4. With the exception of President Nyerere's speech, the proceedings of the recent

World Conference on Agrarian Reform and Rural Development (WCARRD, Rome, July 1979) were a striking example of unanimous participation in conceptual deradicalization.

5. Cf. a similar analysis in Richard Franke and Barbara Chasin, "Science versus Ethics," *Science for the People*, July 1975.

6. Crozier, Huntington, Watanuki, 1975. Noam Chomsky, in *Intellectuals and the State* (Het Wereldvenster Baarn, the Netherlands, 1978) provides a brilliant analysis of intellectuals as "experts in legitimation" and of the institutions they serve as disseminators of the "state religion." His comment on the Trilateral study: "The crisis of democracy to which they refer arises from the fact that during the 1960s, segments of the normally quiescent masses of the population became politically mobilized and began to press their demands, thus creating a crisis, since naturally these demands cannot be met, at least without a significant redistribution of wealth and power, which is not to be contemplated." On "value-oriented intellectuals": "Speaking of our enemies, we despise the technocratic and policy-oriented intellectuals as 'commissars' and 'apparatchiks' and honour the value-oriented intellectuals as the 'democratic dissidents.' At home, the values are reversed."

7. Ponna Wignaraja should be credited with conceptualizing the separate knowledge stocks and the perspective of new "mixes."

8. Details of a seasonal methodology can be found in Pierre Spitz, "Drought, Stocks and Social Classes," UNRISD, 1979.

9. Cf. the presentation by Elise Boulding at the MIT Workshop.

10. John Berger, "Towards Understanding Peasant Experience," *Race & Class*, Vol. 19, No. 4, Spring 1978.

Caveat Emptor
the "transfer" of technology

Dr. Zafrullah Chowdhury is an exceptional man—the product of an upper-class Bengali family who trained as an MD in Dhaka and London and returned to his country during the liberation struggle against Pakistan to care for wounded combatants. He soon after realized that the kind of medicine he had been taught had very little to do with the health problems of the poor rural Bangladeshi majority.

After the war, instead of going into a lucrative urban practice, Chowdhury set up the Gonoshasthaya Kendra—People's Health Center—in the countryside north of Dhaka at Savar; armed with near-zero funds and a boundless faith in the need for decentralized health care serving the real needs of people living in poverty. The Center is now a full-fledged, self-sufficient community reaching out to several tens of thousands of Bangladeshis. It grows its own produce on land previously considered untillable, maintains a school for local children, and has set up an agricultural credit bank and workshops for carpentry, textiles, metal, and leatherworking that provide employment primarily for rural women. A small hospital has been built on the premises, but more important are the paramedics (largely women) who have been trained to cope with most of the health problems encountered in rural Bangladesh, as well as to provide basic obstetrical and family-planning care. They range far and wide in the countryside around Savar, and several subcenters have been established in other parts of the country, staffed in the same way. Chowdhury's latest achievement is a pharmaceuticals factory (largely financed by a Dutch development aid agency and modern in every respect) that will be able to provide basic drugs at a far lower cost than those now sold in Bangladesh by American and British transnational corporations.

None of this has been easy. One can perhaps put up with the austerity of living conditions (Chowdhury's daughter is called Bishti, which means 'rain' in Bengali, because the hut he and his German-born wife Suzanne lived in when the baby was born was awash during the rainy season). The outright hostility of many better-off Bengalis who feel threatened by the GK Center is something else. One of the paramedics was murdered in 1976 by assassins who have been identified but never brought to justice. While I was in Savar, absentee landlords from Dhaka and their hired thugs physically attacked GK workers and tried to bulldoze temporary structures on land the government has promised Chowdhury for an extension of the Center. The landlords have simply noted that the land is worth something after all—and violence is a standard means for gratifying greed in Bangladesh. Chowdhury's next project is to build a teaching hospital where the curriculum will stress not only people-oriented health care but the socio-political conditions that breed poverty and disease.

The following text is the keynote speech Chowdhury asked me to give for the "Transfer of Techology" conference he organized at the GK Center in January 1982. Most of the participants were foreign or Bengali health care professionals; several had important responsibilities in government ministries.

When Dr. Zafrullah Chowdhury invited me to give the keynote speech for the opening of this seminar, I accepted immediately, not only from gratitude for the honor, but especially because it gives me the opportunity, on behalf of all the foreign participants, to salute the remarkable work being done here at Savar by Dr. Chowdhury and all his colleagues. Examples of grassroots, integrated, autonomous and authentic development are all too rare in Third World countries, and while I've often cited Savar as just such an example, I'm enormously pleased at last to see it in operation and also to note that its work is receiving greater and greater support and is being actively encouraged by the people and the authorities of Bangladesh itself.

The greater part of the work of our seminar will be devoted to problems posed by transfers of technology in the fields of health, medicine, and pharmaceuticals. This is as it should be, given the long-term orientation of the Savar Center and its most recent achievement—the resplendent new pharmaceuticals factory. Many other participants will address these topics with great professional competence in the coming days. My task, as defined by Zafrullah Chowdhury, is to try to place the problems of technology transfer in a more general perspective.

Speakers should adhere to one simple, cardinal rule: Talk about what they know. My direct experience of the Third World is limited and this is my first, although I hope not my last, visit to Bangladesh, so I have no pretentions to speaking about the effects of technology transfer in this country. What I hope I know a little more about, as a citizen of one rich, industrialized country and a resident of another, are the nature of Western technology and the plans the ruling elites of the rich countries have for the poor countries as we move towards the end of the twentieth century.

No one here needs to be told that the present world system is in crisis. Poor countries are hit particularly hard—more expensive imported food and energy, crushing debts, dwindling prospects for their own exports and so forth. What I'm concerned with here, however, is how the *rich* nations, and especially their transnational corporations (orTNCs) are reacting to the crisis. Their reactions, as I hope to show, are crucial for the future of the Third World.

In a world of rising costs and diminishing profits, it becomes more important than ever for the industrialized countries and the TNCs to maintain and to reinforce their hegemony over the global economy. They *must*, from their point of view, increase their control over world production and world markets. People who believe that the interventions of TNCs in Third World countries are primarily for the good of those countries; those who believe that these companies have any object besides the enhancement of their own profits are making a serious mistake. The uses—and the abuses—of technology are among the instruments they employ in orchestrating global control.

Let's begin by taking a critical look at our vocabulary itself. Technology is not "transferred"—that is a nice, sanitary, aseptic word. Technology is bought and sold, period. The word "transfer" also implies that "recipient" nations gain real control over a technology deposited in their laps and which then becomes wholly theirs. This, too, is a mistake. Another popular misconception is that "technology" is merely some sort of machinery or apparatus. In reality, technology is never just a *product*. It is also a *process*, and those who buy technology from the West are usually getting a lot more than they bargained for. Let me explore this notion of technology as a process a little more fully.

Present Western technology should not be looked at as a "given" which just happens to be there. A more accurate way to see it is as the *result of several centuries of the history of Western capitalism*. The technology we now use in the West—the same technology that is sold in a stage of greater or lesser obsolescence to the Third World, is by no means determined by pure considerations of efficiency, and it is even less determined by the needs of society as a whole. The technology the West uses is the outcome of a social and political process and of social and political struggles. It embodies relationships between social classes in a particular kind of social organization, and has been developed to serve the needs of those who have come to dominate society.

Unfortunately for the masses of people in the West, the outcome of this centuries-long social and political process has been much less satisfactory—that is, for the vast majority of workers or farmers or service industry employees. During the nineteenth century, the large, centralized factory entirely replaced the small, decentralized (even individual) production units which had previously been the rule. This change took place not so much because the factory system was necessarily more efficient: its outstanding advantage was that it allowed a far greater measure of social control over the workforce.

Who can believe that Western workers would choose of their own free will the "Taylor" system of the assembly line with its speedups, its repetitious, meaningless gestures, and ruthless supervision, dehumanizing and alienating the workforce from the final product of its own labor? Has a later generation of workers "chosen" the technology of industrial robots which is now rapidly eliminating their jobs in the automotive and textile industries, with electronics and others to come? Have farmworkers "chosen" the mechanical lettuce and tomato harvesters developed in direct response to the strikes led by Cesar Chavez? These harvesters are replacing thousands of them in the United States—and will soon do so elsewhere. Have US farmers "chosen" an agricultural technology so expensive that they can no longer meet its costs, so that an average of 800 of them go out of business every week? Have office employees and clerks "chosen" the technology of office automation which will replace up to 40 percent of their numbers before the year 2000 according to recent studies?

Anyone who buys Western technology should understand that he is not just buying a product, but rather a distinct set of social relationships which have now become so embedded in the technology that they are nearly invisible. Along with the technology comes a hierarchical, authoritarian way of organizing production itself—and one which will dispense with human labor whenever feasible. Furthermore, purchasers of technology are buying the end result of our inability in the West to create the desirable society, in spite of all our wealth. I will go even further and say that they are, in effect, buying a kind of *crystallized failure*—the failure of struggles of working people in the West to create full employment, a humane production process, consumption based on socially useful goods and an unpolluted, sustainable environment in which all could live harmoniously. They are also buying conversely, the crystallized success of our ruling elites in imposing productivity and profit as the only goals of human existence. Put another way, the technology we use and are selling to others in the 1980s is certainly not the *only* technology we could devise—just these products, just these processes and no others—inevitable, and somehow foreordained by disembodied, pure reason. The technology we have devised represents a series of *choices* among a whole range of possibilities, and these choices were dictated by a minority whose goal was, is, and always will be its own greater power and profits.

I'm fully aware that this way of looking at present Western technology may surprise you, and that your first reaction may be that millions of people in Bangladesh would consider the lot of a Western worker, small farmer, or employee—even an unemployed one—sheer paradise. Fair enough. But consider for a moment what we *might* have done with our wealth—much of that wealth acquired by exploiting Third World countries.

We could have had more labor-intensive technologies ensuring full employment. Instead, we have at least 30 million unemployed in the OECD countries (Europe and North America).

We could have provided an abundant, varied, and healthy diet for everyone, regardless of social status. Instead we have chemical additives because they contribute to long product life and thus to the profits of the food industry. We have increased our consumption of highly processed junk foods with little or no nutritional value while consumption of fresh produce has declined. There are millions of malnourished people in the United States and Great Britain (especially among old people and minorities) although you might not always recognize this malnutrition because it often shows up as obesity.

We could have had technologies safe to work with. Instead, to give only two examples, there were five deaths and over 500 serious injuries of workers in a single California shipyard in a single recent year. *Business Week* has just reported "a sudden rise in miners' deaths." Occupational health and safety technologies are readily available, but they are also more expensive for companies than sloppy and dangerous methods. Thus thousands more workers in close daily contact with dangerous chemicals or radioactive materials are being slowly poisoned.

We could have had fast, cheap, efficient public transportation. Instead we've given priority to the costly, energy-devouring private automobile. And in Western countries without an adequate national health care system, like the United States, millions of people live in fear of illness, because hospital care—and our hospitals are full of beautiful shiny technology—will eat up their life's savings. Our technologies are not even clean, so we must eat, drink, and breathe the pollutants they leave in the environment.

I could go on giving examples, but my point is that our Western technology—so much admired, it seems, in Third World countries—is far from perfect and serves chiefly those whose incomes put them at the top of the ladder. Obviously I do not wish to do without my telephone or the machine that served to type this speech—but I hope I'm also aware of the harassing working conditions of telephone operators, and that few people who need an electric typewriter as much as I do can afford one.

The slogan "caveat emptor"—"let the buyer beware"—has never been truer than for the case of Third World purchases of Western technology—especially if the buyer does not realize the whole social and cultural history that lies behind the products and processes he is getting. As the Indian scholar A.K.N. Reddy has put it perfectly, technology is a carrier of the genetic code of the society that produced it. Once given, genetic codes are invariable. Those who purchase Western technology had best be prepared to adapt to it, because

Western technology is not going to adapt to them.

An overwhelming share of technological research and development (R&D) is done in the industrialized countries—only about 2 to 3 percent of the world's total R & D capacity is located in the Third World. So it's not surprising that technology transfers are one-way streets, that Third World nations have little influence on the types of technology developed and that their specific needs are not served by this technology.

One can cite such obvious cases as the huge sums expended on military R&D which, in 1979, amounted to $35 billion, with more than half a million scientists and engineers devoting full time to the destruction machine. This represents about a quarter of the world's entire outlay for R&D.

There are non-military dangers as well. When pollution-control laws are passed in the rich countries, we transplant our dirtiest industries to countries where legislation is weak or non-existent. We even use Third World people as guinea pigs for our potentially harmful products—for example, oral contraceptives were tested on Third World women before being marketed in the industrialized countries. Even research that can be classed as oriented to life rather than death is usually irrelevant to Third World needs. Thus the United States spends about nine times as much on cancer and heart disease R&D than the entire world budget for tropical medicine research.

But let's examine the kinds of technology that *are* useful—or at least *used* in the Third World. Remember that this technology is almost exclusively transferred by TNCs directly or by aid programs that call upon these same corporations. In my workroom at home, I have pasted up a small cutting from a corporate advertisement in *Business Week*, because it sums up admirably what TNCs are all about. There are only five words in the ad: "Objective: Maximize Return. Minimize Risk." How do Third World countries fit into this succinct program?

First, they are not allowed to interfere with maximizing return. As the Group of 77 pointed out at the 1979 UN Conference on Science and Technology, 90 percent of the patents granted, supposedly, to Third World countries are, in reality, granted to foreigners—which is to say to subsidiaries of TNCs. Even worse, only about 10 percent of the patents granted are actually used—but so long as they are in force, no one else can use them. The function of the patent system is to *prevent* the generalization of technology developed in the non-industrialized world.

India's experience with TNC technology transfer is instructive, not least because India has a highly sophisticated technological capacity of its own. A recent report by S.K. Goyal of the Indian Institute of Public Administration comes up with the following results: In many industries, including pharmaceuticals, the impact of supposed "technology transfer" is nil, because local affiliates act only as 'bottlers'—they simply repack in small containers bulk drugs imported from the parent firm. Routine assembly of components manufactured elsewhere is the rule in electronics, business machines, and other high-technology product lines—even though India boasts plenty of skilled workers able to manufacture these components.

Whatever advanced technology does come into India tends to stay within the four walls of the TNC subsidiary where Indians work only as laborers and junior technicians. Parent companies take substantial precautions to prevent their equipment and processes from benefiting the country as a whole. The real crunch comes when the parent transfers—so to speak—an item to its subsidiary, because the subsidiary must then make payment for that item out of India's foreign currency reserves at whatever price the company sets. For Imperial Chemical Industries' Indian affiliate, the technical collaboration agreement on polyester fibers involved the affiliate's commitment of £2 million for engineering and design charges made by ICI. This payment does not include a 3.5 percent royalty charge on the value of any and all polyester fibers produced in India in the future. This drain on the country's foreign currency reserves is a recurrent and standard aspect attached to TNC technology transfer. Goyal's team showed that the 189 Indian TNC affiliates that made up the sample not only earned *no* foreign exchange but actually *cost* the country a minimum of $25 million in 1976 alone.

Transfer pricing is a well-developed art for TNCs—they overvalue what they import from the parent firm and undervalue what they export back to it. Thus Goyal concludes: "The practice of exporting goods to parent companies at a loss is obviously an indirect method of transferring resources from India, and the motivation for accelerating such exports is to defeat the spirit of foreign exchange regulations, *not* to promote Indian national interests." This is all part of "maximizing return."

TNCs are not interested in integrating with the rest of a country's economy. They are much more apt to import their raw materials—again paying with precious local foreign exchange—than to encourage raw material production from the local market. But their most negative impact is doubtless on employment.

The number one problem in the Third World today is job creation. Number one—because with millions more jobs, other huge problems like hunger could be virtually eliminated. The International Labour Organisation estimates that at least 300 million Third World people are totally unemployed. The figure swells yearly: in India, for instance, an estimated 100,000 people are added to the potential workforce every *week*. Probably 35-40 million Third World people join this huge army every year.

It is simply not possible, using Western technology, to create anywhere near the billion jobs the Third World will need by the year 2000, for the excellent reason that each industrial job created in the West requires a *minimum* investment of $20,000. A single job made available in US agriculture costs a staggering $400,000 in capital investment. TNCs claim they create employment—and this may be true in a few small enclave countries like Singapore or Hong Kong. But TNCs neglect to tell us how many jobs they *destroy*. A recent ILO study has shown, for example, that in Brazil, from 1970 to 1975, 200 smaller food processing companies went out of business as a direct result of competition from foreign agro-industrial firms. Overall, TNCs create far less employment than is generally supposed and account for only one half of one percent of total Third World jobs, again according to ILO. No one has fully measured their negative influence on employment.

Here is an example from another continent, taken from Stephen Langdon's work on the soap industry in Kenya. Before the advent of TNCs, soap making in Kenya was a highly labor-intensive industry. All stages of production—mixing, molding, drying, cutting, wrapping, warehousing and distributing—were carried out mostly by hand with the aid of simple equipment. Then, the TNCs, including Unilever, arrived with their modern technology, imported, at a price, from the home countries. As the local manager of the Kenyan affiliate of one of these companies explained:

> We have a long history throughout the international firm of being very, very aggressive about the numbers of people we employ . . . It's a corporate objective we have to follow. Labour costs are insignificant here, [less than] one percent of variable costs. And on that basis, we spend an inordinate amount of time searching around for labour reductions. This is a thing we are expected to do. And if I don't do it in my job, then I'm not doing my job right as far as (the parent company) is concerned. So basically, it's an objective which is in conflict with what this country needs.

This manager did indeed eliminate 19 percent of his labor force in five years, in spite of huge increases in sales.

This company, like most others, imports its raw materials instead of using readily available local palm oil, so it gives no incentive to agricultural production.

Any TNC which really wants to make a place for itself in a Third World country has options no local company can possibly match. The relatively small market provided by each individual country is only a tiny part of the firm's overall operation. The TNC can thus afford to practice what is called "deep-pocket financing"— meaning it can undersell local firms, and even sell under its own costs when necessary—until it has captured the market and conveniently eliminated the local competition. When this has occurred, the TNC will naturally put its prices back up to more realistic, not to say monopolistic levels. There are many hidden costs that come with apparently superior technology. Perhaps the most surprising of these is the fact that Third World countries are *themselves* financing the expansion of TNCs. In country after country, one discovers that these firms bring relatively little cash with them, and instead finance their operations from *local* savings. Third World banks consider TNCs more reliable customers than local firms—so the international companies get first go at bank loans at the best credit rates. They thereby indirectly prevent the creation or expansion of national firms which are short of working capital.

In my own work, I've been particularly preoccupied with the harmful effects of the transfer of Western agricultural technology to the Third World. Here I shall limit myself to a single remark. Expensive technology produces expensive food. Someone will have to pay for purchased seeds, chemical fertilizers and pesticides, irrigation equipment, mechanization and the like—and that "someone" is the final consumer as well as the State. A new area known as post-harvest technology—meaning storage and handling—is now very much in fashion. I believe this vogue is partly due to the fact that this part of the food system has been, up to now, only marginally penetrated by foreign agribusiness, and that companies see this as a potentially profitable activity; as a way of gaining more control over food systems as a whole. In this sense, post-harvest technology investment opportunities could be to the 1980s what the Green Revolution was to the 60s and 70s. Be that as it may, we can be sure that centralized storage, using costly silos and warehousing as opposed to family, village, or regional level storage; adds at least 20 percent to the final cost of the stored food, according to an FAO expert. This kind of cost increase is enough to price the poorest consumers out of the market— the very people who are already suffering from malnutrition.

Whether we're talking about food, health, or any other vital area, Western technology has these two characteristics: it favors central- ization—meaning cities—and it caters to demand expressed in purchasing power rather than to human needs. The handsomely equipped Third World hospital, rivaling anything in the United States or France, but eating up so much of the State health budget that little is left over for the majority in the countryside, is an excellent example of the centralization syndrome. The introduction of profitable processed foods or cola drinks only a minority can afford (and which are, in any event, an expensive way of consuming empty calories) puts technological expertise to work for socially useless ends. From capital's viewpoint, however, human beings are divided into two groups: those who can pay and those who cannot. The first group is called consumers. The needs of the second are not even noticed. This is how one "maximizes return."

The second part of my *Business Week* ad says "minimize risk." TNCs have no intention of giving up real control over the production process, nor of sacrificing any profits to be made, so host countries that welcome their technology should understand that they will be unable to challenge the way the corporations have decided to organize production. An illustration is the electronics industry in Asia. I've seen these operations in Malaysia's Free Trade Zones and it's obvious the companies have very little fixed investment; they could pull out tomorrow with no loss if it became more profitable to produce elsewhere. Meanwhile, they employ young women from about age 16 to 25—after that, the women's eyesight becomes too feeble to continue working all day through a microscope. Then a fresh younger group takes over. A recent study by the Max Planck Institute in Germany indicates that the German work-year in electronics is 1800 hours, whereas in South Korea, it comes to 2800 hours for equal or superior productivity and, naturally, at far lower wages. This is just common exploitation. But TNC insistence on a docile, risk-free workforce also carries a cost for the whole society. As the Max Planck study points out: "It is not surprising that the list of those countries in which free production zones and world market factories are in operation . . . is to a great extent similar to a list of those countries in which labour unions are either prohibited or greatly hindered and in which strikes are largely suppressed." Denial of labor rights—even human rights—and TNC investment tend to go together.

Even when countries are willing to create what the companies blandly call a 'favorable climate for investment', or, more baldly stated, to carry out repression, the host country may find little residual benefit in the way the TNC has decided to organize production. The firms' strategies are, as their name indicates, *trans*national. Some of the more powerful TNCs with a great many subsidiaries have invented a new technological twist. The Ford Motor Company calls it "complementation." This strategy consists in producing only one element of the final product in each national subsidiary—say gearboxes or chassis—and assembling these elements subsequently in a third country. Ford is moving towards the "global car" and when this strategy has reached maturity, there will be at least two countries manufacturing each vital component. This not only creates a strike-proof industry: It means that if a country should decide to nationalize the factory, it will not get an automobile plant. It will get nothing but a gearbox or chassis plant of absolutely no interest to anyone but Ford. Following a trip to nine Asian countries, Henry Ford announced, "Complementation holds far more promise for the region than adherence to old-style purchasing, assembly and manufacturing methods." From his point of view of risk-minimization, I'm sure that's true.

To sum up, technology transfer is much more often than not labor-displacing and dependency-creating—just the traps Third World countries should most avoid. Many countries believe they are buying independence when they buy technology packages. But because the firms keep control over the *way* this technology is used, independence is not what they get. Rather, as the German scholar Dieter Ernst has said, "A strategy which seeks to strengthen national political and economic autonomy through aggressive acquisition of high technology may, paradoxically, lead not to greater technological autonomy but to greater dependence at a qualitatively higher level."

There is a final point I do not wish to gloss over. Just as we must understand the ruling elites of rich countries whose choices determine technology types for both rich and poor, so must we confront the problem of ruling elites in the Third World. There is no doubt that many of their members may find an interest—either financial or in terms of career—in cooperating with the purveyors of unadapted and unadaptable technology. There is also no doubt that these elites generally insist that priority be given to luxury goods and to the cities where most of them live. They may give little or no thought to the needs of their poorer compatriots. We can all recite tales of corruption, bribery, or just plain deals in which TNCs and local authorities and businessmen work hand-in-glove for mutual interest and profit.

I still believe, however, that many members of these elites are true nationalists and are working for the betterment of their countries under extremely difficult conditions. It is to such people that I should like to direct my closing remarks.

By the very fact that rich countries are rich, their technology carries with it an aura of invincibility and of perfection. It *must* be good since it has, apparently, brought wealth to the nations that produced it. This is a myth, but a very powerful one. The existence of this myth proves that rich countries do not merely dominate our economy. They also dominate our concepts and ideas—and we are all to some extent the victims of this dominant ideology. The power of this ideology also testifies to the poverty of developed country scholarship. As scholars, we haven't demystified our own societies and our own technology. It is with this belief that I devote much of my own time to a critique of the dominant agribusiness technologies in hopes that such work may in some small way help to clear the air and prepare the ground for scientific and technological renewal in the Third World.

You may have found my remarks excessively negative, but they, too, have been aimed at air-clearing and ground-preparing. I do not wish to make a plea here for so-called "appropriate" or "alternative" technology in the classic way this debate has been presented. Third World countries are right to be wary of "appropriate" technology when this term actually means "second-rate." "Appropriate" technology can be a way of allowing the same old TNCs—or their younger sisters—to introduce technology which may be smaller-scale but which is just as dependency-creating. Some countries can't afford the biggest and brightest, but they can still contribute to corporate profits at their own level. And this technology does not even necessarily benefit the poorest people in society as the recent development of biogas plants in India has demonstrated.

What I *do* hope is *first*, that Third World decision makers will take a far more critical look at what they assume to be advanced technology and recognize all the hidden costs—including the social and cultural costs—the purchase of this technology entails.

Second, I hope they will foster and encourage on every possible occasion local solutions to local problems. The pharmaceuticals factory at Savar is one excellent example, and because it is already effective and can become even more effective, we may be absolutely certain the TNC drug firms in Bangladesh will fight back. I look forward to learning that this fight has been won by Savar and Savar's supporters.

Third, those of us who would like to see authentic and autonomous development in the Third World—the kind of development which cannot be accomplished under the present regime of dependency—do not say Small is Beautiful or Big is Beautiful but that Choice is Beautiful. Every technological decision should be aimed at giving the country the maximum number of options. In my view, the most direct road to greater flexibility and to the creation of wealth and a decent livelihood for all is through the choice of decentralized, labor-intensive technologies. But "decentralized" and "labor-intensive" do not necessarily mean "simple." Some of these choices may, indeed, be far more sophisticated than anything the West is in a position to offer. This would be the case, for example, with agricultural technologies based on polyculture, crop interactions, and environment-enhancing crop protection techniques. By comparison, Western agricultural methods are extremely crude.

Advocates of autonomous development further believe that there are enormous reservoirs of hidden creativity in the Third World that are presently stifled or going to waste. Allowing this creativity to surface means taking the knowledge of peasants and workers into account and building upon it to improve existing techniques. Such an approach demands a great deal of political courage, because it conflicts with so many established interests at home and abroad.

If I may make one last recommendation to technological decision makers it is this: The next time someone calls you a technocrat, be proud of the title. Remember that it comes from the Greek "kratia" or "kratos" meaning "power" or "strength." This power and strength can serve the cause of outsiders and place your country under the yoke of dependency. But with the help of your people, it can also make you free.

The SNOB Theory of
Underdevelopment

Comic relief time. Or at least a satirical tone for a serious subject. This piece appeared in Development Forum, *June 1982, "the single regular publication of the United Nations system in the field of economic and social development," under the title "An Invitation to be Offended."* Development Forum *does not require permission to reprint, but I thank them anyway and change the title back to "The SNOB Theory of Underdevelopment."*

"Of course, poor Mr. James never *did* meet the right people."

English dowager, commenting on Henry James, upper-class American anglophile novelist who took British nationality

"Breastfeeding is for savages."

African doctor

I hope to be among the first to alienate nearly all my friends by bringing up in the most public and tasteless manner a subject not discussed in well-bred 'development' intellectual circles, except in whispers and with intimates, after midnight.

If you too are a believer, but afraid to come out of the closet, perhaps this may give you the courage to talk openly about SNOB. The acronym stands for Social Naiveté of Behavior or Simple Necessities of Business, depending on which side you're looking at. Those who espouse the SNOB theory hold dear the motto, "Nothing So Blind as a Colonized Mind."

SNOB is an idea whose time has come, because exploitation in the postcolonial world is a tricky business. No more rounding up the natives and telling them to produce, or else. No more dumping cheap goods on vassalized countries' markets to ruin local cottage industries. Tough times for business, these. But hardly desperate. There's more than one way to skin a cat—or a Third World country and its citizens. The SNOB method, properly employed, not only yields higher profits but provides more perverse satisfaction to its practitioners than common or garden domination.

The theoretical underpinnings of SNOB have been known for centuries and its practical applications are universal. SNOB's guiding principle is that human beings tend to imitate those they perceive as their social superiors. Adepts regard Molière, immortal author of *Le Bourgeois Gentilhomme*, as their greatest ancestor. Literati would add Proust, creator of Madame Verdurin and other unforgettable characters, to the Pantheon; while academics may recall Gabriel Tarde, early sociologist and neglected author of *The Laws of Imitation* (1895). Americans, more succinctly, may recite, if pressed, "Oh carry me back to Boston/ The home of the bean and the cod/ Where the Lodges speak only to Cabots/ And the Cabots speak only to God."

SNOB in its early expressions was thus an intra-cultural phenomenon, operating within closed frontiers. Those who attempted to cross rigid class barriers were objects of ridicule because they tried so earnestly to imitate their "betters" and did such a rotten job of it.

With the rise of consumer culture, advertisers and merchandisers were quick to see the goldmine SNOB promised. Calvert whiskey's "Men of Distinction" campaign of the 1950s was a classic that changed the image of a decidedly lower-class brand. With transnational capitalism, SNOB began to creep across frontiers and now flourishes wherever insecure people gather: e.g., one can sell *very* expensive raincoats to Americans using pictures of Lady X and Lord Y strolling across lawns obviously trod by the same family for the past five-hundred years.

Harmless, you may say, and a further illustration that a fool and his money are soon parted. So, alas, are a fool and his culture. As SNOB steals from North to South; from the ex-colonists to the ex-colonized, it erodes the cultural topsoil and washes it away to sea, leaving barren ground that will readily soak up a variety of products profitable to their purveyors, if not to their purchasers.

The goal of the practicing corporate (or development agency) SNOB is to enroll Third World bourgeoisies in the brotherhood: they can be counted on to carry along their own masses. In winning hearts and minds, modern SNOBs wouldn't dream of using bombs and napalm when training programs, foundation grants, marketing experts, and mass media work so much more effectively. The fun of the game is to make the victim *want* your _____ . The blank may be filled in with "dangerous pharmaceuticals," "plastic shoes," "infant formula," "soft drinks," *ad libitum*; and easily extended to include "hospital-based health care," "educational system," "agricultural techniques," etc.

This has proven almost too simple. The only element that adds spice and subtlety to the mind-colonizing game is this: The target population must be encouraged to abandon its own authentic culture in favor of a lower-middle class, Western, wholly commercialized ersatz. Third World elites must not, with very rare exceptions, be allowed to witness or to participate in the culture of Western *upper* classes, for the very reason that this upper-class culture is often *uncannily close* to the one the conditioned victim must learn to despise as 'backward' and 'inferior' in his own country, for obvious commercial reasons.

The point can be illustrated in an area which is at once a basic need and an intensely cultural activity: food and eating. Witness the sleight of hand involved in the shift from an authentic Third World culture to raw Western consumerism aped by Third World bourgeoisies and back full circle to the values of the Occidental upper crust.

Breastfeeding

- "Savages" breastfeed, as the quoted African doctor puts it.
- Western masses and *nouveaux riches* (and not so *riches*) Third Worlders bottlefeed with infant formula.
- Upper-class, educated Western women breastfeed.

Shapes and Sizes

- "Natives" are thin because they work hard and often go hungry.
- Lower and middle class Westerners are often obese—as are rich Third World wives—living proof their husbands can afford to stuff them.
- Rich Westerners are slender—indeed they may spend as much money losing weight as putting it on.

State of the Plate

- Peasants eat, necessarily, whole unprocessed food because they can ill afford anything else.
- *Hoi polloi* in the rich countries and the rich in poor countries are great customers for junk food, as transnational food processing companies have learned to their advantage. Here, too, Third World bourgeoisies have played their destined role of bringing much of the rest of the (far poorer) population to the joys of commerciogenic malnutrition.
- Upper-class Westerners now pay premium prices for whole, unprocessed foods.

Meals versus Food Contacts

- Peasants serve their fare in hand-crafted clay, wooden, or metal utensils, and they eat as a group—family or clan.

- Plastic and pyrex prevail among the commoners who, in the West, may rarely enjoy a family meal. In the United States, "eating" is now sociologically described in terms of "food contacts"—as many as 15 to 20 a day in the snack civilization.
- Avant-garde Westerners seek out hand-crafted utensils and are the only ones who can still afford the time for leisurely dining and commensality (a variant of this is the business lunch). If they are especially chic, some of the food will come from their own gardens, just like Third World peasants.

It would be nice to make a similar case for peasant polyculture (mixes of different kinds of crops and animals) as opposed to standardized, vulnerable Western monoculture and back—but the environmental movement has not yet forced industrialized countries to recognize the importance of biological complexity in farming systems. The Third World, naturally, is working flat out to transform its polycultural systems into much riskier monocultural ones.

Time lags complicate the whole SNOB issue. Third World bourgeoisies also imitate Western styles of ten or fifteen years ago, now totally passé in their places of origin. Look at the young blades in Asia who think they are fashion plates in bell-bottom trousers no Western kid (even a lower-class one) would be caught dead wearing today.

I believe SNOBism is here to stay. That is why I propose, on the principle, "if you can't beat 'em, join 'em," that we *encourage* Third World imitation of Western mores, but that we make some effort in the direction of social equality. Like poor Henry James, Third World elites never *do* meet the right people. Perhaps the United Nations could open a new agency, designed to receive Third World opinion makers, with branches in the more desirable Western countries.

It would be partially staffed with volunteers from the best families and would devote itself to the display of authentic upper-class Western lifestyles. Trendy New York hostesses could lecture on how they serve unpolished rice and perfect vegetable terrines (nothing quite so déclassé as a steak nowadays) at their most fashionable dinners. Their husbands would explain that 'nobody' watches television or buys *anything* plastic when a natural substance is available. Elegant Britishers would put down polyester and nylon; Scandinavian industrialists' daughters would carry on pleasant conversations while breastfeeding their babies. French intellectuals would take participants to film festivals to watch esthetic movies about workers and peasants. The possibilities are endless . . . .

Who knows? Western corporations could lose a few marginal markets, but Third World elites might begin to feel secure in their own traditions.

A Knowledge of Hunger

In 1981, Nicole Ball published a remarkable critical bibliography titled World Hunger: a Guide to the Economic and Political Dimensions* to which she *kindly asked me to write a foreword. As soon as I saw the text, I realized that whatever needed to be said about hunger itself had already been said by Ball. The only path left open to the writer of a foreword was to make something of the fact that the bibliography's 3,000 and some entries actually existed—i.e., that hunger has been, to say the least, a problem very much in the academic limelight in recent years. Thus I tried to talk about the peculiar ambiguity of the 'hunger-and-development' scholar, his/her place in the power structures, and how we might "apply ourselves to transforming the contents of future bibliographies into explosive devices and instruments of liberation." This foreword, which is reprinted here with the kind permission of the publishers, also appeared in the Institute for Policy Studies' collective volume titled* First Harvest, *1983.*

---

*Libraries in particular should be urged to purchase Ball's work: available from ABC Clio Press, Riviera Campus, 2040 Alameda Padre Serra, Box 4397, Santa Barbara, CA 93103.

I nclusion of this bibliography on world hunger in the War/Peace Bibliography Series published by ABC-Clio is a clear recognition that hunger and underdevelopment are forms of violence and sources of conflict. Nicole Ball, who prepared this outstanding instrument for researchers, the first of its kind, subtitled her work *A Guide to the Economic and Political Dimensions.* This in itself is a step forward for scholarship. Indeed, until recently, hunger was generally regarded as a technical problem, amenable to technical solutions, or at most as the temporary malfunctioning of an essentially viable world economic system. Ball, both in her general introduction and her headings for subsections, correctly guides the reader toward those studies which examine hunger as a function of poverty and poverty as a function of fundamentally inequitable power structures both within and between nations. She has done this as competently as she has collected the source materials—which is saying a great deal—and this foreword need not restate her fully justified conclusions.

Ball has also given us an important tool for examining how the allocation of power influences scholarship itself. A bibliography is not merely a convenience to the general reader and a time-saver for academics in libraries. It is also, particularly in the present case, a contribution to the sociology of knowledge—a documentary record of the ways in which scholars and institutions have viewed one of the great issues of their time. If we try to analyze this bibliography as an object in itself—concentrating not, as most of the following entries do, on poverty and hunger, but on what has been said about them—we may ask a few basic questions conducive to healthy critical thinking.*

First question: Who is doing the talking? Which is to say, who is in a position to publish books, monographs, and scholarly articles on various aspects of world hunger and underdevelopment? Despite Ball's careful inclusion of many Third World sources and authors (a

Reprinted from *World Hunger: A Guide to the Economic and Political Dimensions* by Nicole Ball by permission of ABC-Clio, Inc.

*This is the approach taken by Pierre Spitz, to whom I am much indebted, in "Silent Violence: Famine and Inequality" a study of the significance of the views on inequality within and between nations, especially the views of those in a position to institutionalize violence against the poor and to deprive them of their right to food.

rarity in the bibliographical genre), she herself would be the first to admit that those who publish are mostly Westerners. In other words, certain groups have the power to make their views known. Whatever their personal hardships may have been, chronic hunger has surely not been among them. Just as there were no Third World peasant representatives at the 1974 World Food Conference or at the 1979 World Conference on Agrarian Reform and Rural Development, so there are no hungry people speaking from direct and painful experience in these pages. Although it is perhaps not necessary to have known physical or social deprivation to write about them, one should still note that the works listed here proceed from a particular kind of external knowledge and that a collection of people with university educations, frequently PhDs, are, by any standards, part of a privileged minority. This does not, of course, predestine them to adopt the point of view characteristic of the group which they belong, but statistically speaking, they are likely to share common intellectual or class biases and to ignore certain problems, not out of personal malice but because these problems may appear unworthy of notice or remain wholly invisible. Non-Western authors are not exempt from such tendencies, particularly when they have received their education under Western auspices.

These observations may become more persuasive when we ask a second question: What—and whom—are these authors talking about? The subject matter of most "development" writing is more circumscribed than such a copious bibliography suggests. The disregard for the specific problems of Third World women in the male-dominated literature is one striking example; the absence of consideration for peasants' specific agricultural knowledge as opposed to that of "scientific experts" is another. Cause for even more serious concern is the proportion of research devoted to the study of poor and powerless groups. This choice of subject is generally accompanied by a lack of interest in the doings of the rich and powerful in the same society. Research directed exclusively toward the victims of hunger, rather than toward their relationships with the powerful (locally, nationally, and internationally), helps to mask the basic reasons for the poor's lack of access to food. Such a focus may help to explain the success of the "overpopulation-is-the-cause-of-hunger" school. (Here, had Ball wished to provide an exhaustive bibliography, she might have needed roughly a third of the pages of this volume.) By placing the hunger problem squarely in the laps, figuratively and literally, of the people having the babies, scholarship has deflected attention from the responsibilities of the "haves" to the plight of the "have-nots," thus obviating the need for any changes in present power arrangements. The sheer weight of the literature devoted to topics that are at best marginal in explaining, much less attacking, the root causes of poverty also stifles academic and public debate and creates confusion in the minds of the general public. And yet, in spite of such obvious cases of scholarly bias or blindspots, a significant portion of the academic establishment would still have us believe that the social sciences are objective, or in the jargon of the trade, "value-free"; that the social scientist is an impartial, politically neutral expert. Here a paraphrase of Orwell seems called for: All social scientists are neutral, but they are more neutral toward some social groups than toward others.

Third question: What goals does research serve, and whose goals are they? At one level, not so trivial as it might first appear, it serves the interests of the people publishing. All of us listed in these pages must live with the uncomfortable truth that at least a part of our own livelihood derives from the existence of the suffering of others. Our published works and inclusion in catalogs like this one may help us gain income or prestige and a higher rung on the career ladder. This in itself should cause us to feel in some way accountable to the Third World countries and people who provided raw material for our research or at least to our colleagues on the three poor continents. This, unfortunately, is not often the case. As of 1979, a massive publication on the Sahelian countries, compiled by a prestigious US university team, was unavailable to scholars in Upper Volta. This is not merely a lack of academic courtesy, but a demonstration of the social and political priorities and loyalties of mainstream scholarship.

What of the goals of research and the accountability of intellectuals at a more general level? Just as most work done in the physical and natural sciences ultimately serves production, so much social science eventually contributes to social control.

Research is intellectual production, and like other kinds of production, must be paid for. The government or international agencies and large foundations that fund scholarship have their own economic and political vision of what constitutes the desirable society. Viewed in this light, it is doubtful that (as Ball states in her introduction) "foundations sponsoring the HYV research and the plant scientists whom they employed *could have chosen* to address the question of developing 'peasant-biased' high-yielding varieties of seeds rather than the 'landlord-biased' varieties which ultimately became the basis of the 'seed-fertilizer [green] revolution'" (emphasis added). This revolution was, in fact, an alternative to agrarian reform, which implies redistribution of power: it was a means of increasing food production without upsetting entrenched interests (as well as a means of providing increased revenues to the Western firms supplying industrial inputs). The choices made by research sponsors were, from their point of view, altogether logical ones; the alternative of peasant-biased varieties was probably not even imagined, much less given serious consideration. Academic defenders of the Green Revolution— and they were legion—rarely bothered to ask "Production by whom? and for whom?"; questions which have now been answered, for example, in the case of India where substantial grain reserves exist partly because half the population is too poor to buy them.

Knowledge costs money, and money is not thrown away by those who dispose of it. It is no accident that our libraries are filled with studies on the hungry and poverty-stricken of the Third World. Cynically but realistically put, the more one knows about those who may, in desperation, become restive and dangerous, the better tools one possesses for keeping them in check. Scholarship may also, wittingly or unwittingly, serve purely commercial interests. One fears, for instance, that the current vogue for studying "appropriate technology" may become a vehicle for introducing new dependency-creating products in societies where incomes are inadequate for the purchase of expensive high-technology goods, but which can contribute to Western corporate interests at their own level.

Finally, social scientists can also function as promoters of particular ideologies and help to create a climate in which development strategies devised by the powerful may be pursued without hindrance or criticism. Intellectuals, as Noam Chomsky has put it, are "experts in legitimation" and in packaging concepts so that they will sell, even if the wrappings conceal shoddy and adulterated merchandise.

There are basically three paradigms or models in the literature of development and hunger alleviation. The first is the "growth/trickle-down" model, more fully described by Ball, which seeks the increase of gross national product through industrialization and by concentrating on those elements of society supposedly most "modern" or "entrepreneurial" (poor peasants, in contrast, are "backward" or "traditional," although it is no longer considered fashionable to say so). The accumulated wealth of these "modernizing elites" will, eventually, also benefit the worse-off. This model encourages the import of foreign capital and technology (as well as the implantation of multinational corporations) and assumes that the development process in the Third World should imitate the one that occurred in the now industrialized Western countries. Economic and social control is concentrated in the hands of the classes which act as motors of growth. This paradigm presupposes harmony: harmony at the national level (the elites will somehow want to share their advantages with their poorer compatriots, towards whom their attitude is essentially benevolent); harmony at the international level, also called "interdependence" (the present world system is beneficial to all nations which should trade according to the principles of "comparative advantage"). Due to its generally recognized failure, this first model has lately been perceived as badly in need of a facelift. This has been undertaken but is largely rhetorical. New keywords are *basic needs* and *participation*, but as defined by experts, mostly from developed countries. Deprived people are neither to be consulted as to their needs nor allowed to participate to the degree that they might demand fundamental changes in existing patterns of income or power distribution.

The second model is based on "dependency theory" which holds that there is a center (the rich countries, with the United States as the center of the center) and a periphery (the Third World); and that the former has consistently exploited the latter since colonial times. The goal of development is thus to correct this historic and ongoing imbalance through the use of measures summed up in the New International Economic Order (NIEO) strategy: fair and stable prices for Third World raw materials, free access to Northern markets for industrial goods, state control over multinational corporations' practices, alleviation of debt, etc. This model also rests on an assumption of global interdependence, but stresses that serious adjustments will have to be made in the world system so that all nations can benefit and achieve that mutuality of interest which does not yet exist. This is the stance from which nearly all Third World governments (the so-called Group of 77) argue in international negotiations.

The third model does not deny the need for an NIEO, but tries to enrich this concept with a class analysis. The world is not merely divided into rich/powerful and poor/relatively powerless nations: all countries, including the rich ones, are characterized by a dominating and a dominated class (each, of course, with its own subdivisions). The NIEO is an incomplete solution to the problems of hunger and underdevelopment because nothing guarantees that increased national revenues will benefit the poor more than marginally. In the third model, the goal of development is not merely greater equality between states, but the decent livelihood and dignity of all human beings. Unlike the first model, this approach assumes not harmony but conflict. Third world elites will not give up their privileges without a struggle and will meanwhile prevent any substantial advantages from trickling down. Rich nations will continue to exploit poor ones, but industrialized country elites will also support their Third World counterparts so that this exploitation may more conveniently continue.

Advocates of the third model see hope for the Third World not in the greater integration of the less developed countries into the world system but in their greater independence from it. They call for self-reliance—the full use of all local material and human resources—

before asking for outside help and for a fundamental redistribution of power as the only way to end hunger and misery. *Basic needs*, yes, but as defined by the communities concerned; not so much *participation* as empowerment—the capacity to control those decisions which most affect one's life.

Has scholarship anything to contribute to the emergence and the enforcement of the third model (for which my own bias will be obvious)? Development students, researchers, and writers must address the needs of the most deprived and must be accountable for the work they produce. Students who see such accountability as an intellectual and moral imperative can begin by approaching the material listed here with their critical faculties on full alert and by asking the kinds of questions we have sketched here: Is the study part of the "conventional wisdom," or does it try to take an opposing or unpopular point of view? Where does it stand in relation to the above three models, i.e., to power? Does it presume harmony and proceed in a social and political vacuum? Could the work contribute to increasing the knowledge—and thus the manipulative capacity—of national or international elites?

The reader, and especially the writer, should not forget that researchers, too, stand somewhere in the power structure. Their work can be used by the rich against the poor, but one may also hope, vice versa. Why not turn our sights toward those who hold control, with a view to giving a clearer understanding of their activities to those whose lives they affect? This is often a difficult task, for the well-endowed are less vulnerable to scholarly scrutiny than those who have no choice but to let themselves be studied; we should accept this as a challenge.

The mass of scholarship listed here represents an incalculable number of hours devoted to examining various aspects of world hunger, and while all of us have been writing, the relative and absolute numbers of hungry and destitute people have vastly increased. It is time we ask ourselves why, as scholars, we are still discussing poverty and want, and apply ourselves to transforming the contents of future bibliographies into explosive devices and instruments of liberation.

About the Author

Susan George is a Senior Fellow of the Transnational
Institute, the international program of the Institute for
Policy Studies. She is author of *How the Other Half Dies: The
Real Reasons for Hunger* (Penguins, 1976 and Allanheld,
Osmun, 1977), *Feeding the Few: Corporate Control of Food*
(Institute for Policy Studies, 1979), *Les Stratèges de la Faim*
(doctoral dissertation, Grounauer, 1981), and *Food for
Beginners* (with illustrations by Nigel Paige, Writers and
Readers, 1982). Susan George has written on food politics
and world hunger for *Le Monde Diplomatique, Food Monitor,
Multinational Monitor, Economic and Political Weekly*, and other
publications, and is a regular columnist for the monthly
Africasia; she works with non-governmental organizations
and the media to popularize the struggle against world
hunger and to promote understanding of its causes; and
she has served as a consultant to UNESCO, The United
Nations University, the Economic Commission for Europe
of the United Nations, the International Union of Food
Workers, and the Government of Nicaragua.

RELATED TITLES PUBLISHED BY
WRITERS AND READERS.

SICILIAN LIVES
by Danilo Dolci

When Danilo Dolci, peace worker, organizer, educator, first arrived in 1952 in Trappeto, a village of peasants and fishermen in western Sicily, there were no streets, just mud and dust, not a single drugstore, not even a sewer. (In fact, the local dialect didn't even have a word for sewer.) Like other Sicilians, the villagers, seen by many Italians as "bandits," "dirt-eaters," and "savages," had, in effect, been mute for centuries.

Dolci's years of work in Sicily broke this silence, and the result is Sicilian Lives, a book which reveals the intimate experiences and perceptions of a wide range of Sicilians, rural and urban, through voices that are sometimes frightening, but always fascinating and unexpected. What does a man who makes his meagre living catching snails and frogs think when he looks into the eyes of the thousandth frog he's about to kill? What does a pickpocket think as he's about to knock over his mark? An organizer faced with the threat of Mafia violence?

"Nobody reading this book can fail to be struck by what the stories reveal about the intolerable conditions, flagrant injustice and endemic violence imposed upon the lives of the tellers."
John Berger from the Foreword

Paperback	**£4.95**	0 906495 87	3
Cased Edition	**£9.95**	0 906495 86	3

Writers and Readers

FOOD FOR BEGINNERS
by Susan George & Nigel Paige

"The illustrations by Nigel Paige illuminate the persistent logic of Susan George's writing. Students, as well as mature 'aid' people will be stimulated by the solutions proposed."
Brian W. Walker
Director General, Oxfam

"A cutting exposé of the exploitation and inequality, both national and international, that cause so much of the hunger in the world."
Paul Harrison
Author of **Inside the Third World** and
The Third World Tomorrow

"I am fascinated by the facts and figures given with regard to food production and distribution ... This book will go some way towards remedying the defects."
Rt. Rev. Trevor Huddleston, CR

Paperback **£3.95** 0 906495 85 7
Cased Edition **£6.95** 0 906495 84 9

A SEVENTH MAN
by John Berger & Jean Mohr

"Why do the industrial European countries depend for their production on importing 22 million hands and arms to do the most menial work? Why are the owners of those arms and hands treated like replaceable parts of a machine? What compels the migrant worker to leave his village and accept this humiliation?

Today the migrant worker experiences, within a few years, what the working population of every industrial city once experienced over generations. To consider his life – its material circumstances and his inner feelings – is to be brought face to face with the fundamental nature of our present societies and their histories. The migrant is not on the margin of modern experience; he is absolutely central to it.

To bring this experience directly to the reader we needed political analysis and poetry. We needed to quote economists and to write fiction. Above all we needed photographs. Jean Mohr and I have continued the experiment begun in 'A Fortunate Man' and continued in 'Ways of Seeing'. We hope that the way this book is made – not just what it states – may question any preconceptions about its subject."

John Berger

Paperback **£4.95**   0 906495 90 3

A DYING COLONIALISM
by Frantz Fanon

In this collection of political essays, Fanon gives expression to the vast complexity of the life of colonized peoples. He shows how the colonized man 'feels himself emptied, without life, in a bodily struggle with death . . .' and he exposes the close relationship which exists between colonized and colonizer.

Frantz Fanon's name has for two decades now been identified with an indictment of colonialism and a commitment to liberation struggles in the Third World.

Studies in a Dying Colonialism was written in the fifth year of the Algerian Revolution. Throughout these years, Fanon worked as a psychiatrist in an Algerian hospital. In this book he not only identifies the justice of the Algerian cause and analyzes the relations between colonial and subject peoples, but also shows how the experience of nationalist struggle radically altered traditional attitudes to the family, women, technology and medicine. In short, how a new socialist nation was formed.

At a time when the developing world is dominated by revolutionary struggles, Fanon's study continues to be of prime importance.

"The Third World finds itself and speaks to itself through his voice."

Jean Paul Sartre

"Among the most enlightening books yet to be written on the psychology of the revolutionary spirit in the developing world."

African Forum

Paperback   **£2.50**   0 904613 98 4

Writers and Readers

These titles are available at good bookshops or, in case of difficulty,
may be obtained by post from:

Writers and Readers Bookshop
144 Camden High Street
London NW1 0NE

If you would like to receive our current catalogue listing all our
titles, please write to the above and enclose a s.a.e.